THE ACCIDENTAL CHURCH

CHURCH
alive

The Accidental
Church

CAROL HATHORNE

KINGSWAY PUBLICATIONS
EASTBOURNE

ISBN 1 84291 101 5

*Some names in this book have been changed to
protect the identities of individuals.*

Published by
KINGSWAY COMMUNICATIONS LTD
Lottbridge Drove, Eastbourne BN23 6NT, England.
Email: books@kingsway.co.uk

Book design and production for the publishers by
Bookprint Creative Services, P.O. Box 827, BN21 3YJ, England.
Printed in Great Britain.

Contents

Foreword

This book tells a story, and throws down a challenge.

The story is a true one, and reflects two of Carol Hathorne's gifts. The first is the kind of pastoral care that sees an apparently intractable problem facing a community, and does something about it. The second is the ability to see what happens as a developing story, and to turn it into an attractive narrative.

The combination is a kind of contemporary Acts of the Apostles, in which a new form of church emerges. This church attracts people who do not normally think of themselves as religious, and it offers prayer and spiritual growth as well as effective social work. As in Acts, there are creative tensions between this new church and the existing congregation.

The challenge of the book lies in its title: *The Accidental Church*. It is a church which comes into being unexpectedly when people are responding to a crying need in the community, rather than trying to ensure the survival of the church in the conventional way. The book tells how new talents are released, and many people want to become involved.

The future of the church depends on adventurous initiatives like the one described in this book. It will be a church that experiments with new forms of meeting and worship. Instead of beginning by demanding strict standards of believing and behaving, this new church will begin by offering outsiders a new experience of belonging. That is close to the stories told about Jesus and the early church in the New Testament. This book tells how it can happen in an ordinary, middle-of-the-road and unglamorous parish in the English Midlands.

Michael Bourke
Bishop of Wolverhampton

Introduction

Most people have never heard of Chadsmoor. The ones who have might tell you that it's an ex-mining village in Staffordshire, almost midway between Cannock (where the late Dusty Springfield made her singing debut at the local Danillo cinema) and Hednesford, once famous for a first division football team.

Despite waves of unemployment and urban deprivation, Chadsmoor retains some features of a less stressful bygone age. There is a wool shop that sells children's dance shoes, a hardware store where goods are put on display outside every day, a greengrocer's where there is time to chat, and a seed merchant's, selling dried, mysterious compounds for garden and allotment, and treats for dogs and cats.

Like an animated child's drawing of a row of shops, there is, dotted along the main street of Chadsmoor, an incongruity of hairdresser's, small tatty supermarkets and Asian restaurants. In addition, the village has two fish and chip shops, a Chinese takeaway and three pubs.

Round the corner, in a magnificently maintained Victorian time warp, there sits the Church of England junior school, a hundred years old and rightly proud of its red brick façade and corridors dripping coat pegs. Here, traditionally, those leaving nearby Kingsway infants are received and nurtured by some of the same teachers who taught their parents.

Chadsmoor has three places of worship, each with its

own distinctive congregation: Bethany Baptist, which is warm and lively in spite of ageing members and no regular pastor; Chadsmoor Methodist, once known as the 'Shropshire Chapel' because of the re-located miners who built it; and St Chad's Anglican church, built in 1892, a brick building with a flattened Mediterranean tower that belies the arctic temperature inside.

In the last census, the population of Chadsmoor was estimated at 6,000. On an average Sunday morning, only twenty people attend St Chad's Church.

1

The Unexpected Visitor

'I was a stranger and you welcomed me.'
(Matthew 25:35)

'Can you help me, please?' The young man who rang the vicarage doorbell that rainy afternoon in January looked vaguely familiar. Aged about twenty-five, he had a thin, rather blotchy red face and almost grotesquely glittering glasses, behind which his dark eyes looked huge and desperate. He wore no coat, and the shoulders of his grey sweater steamed in the heavy downpour. His dark hair was plastered to his head, and as he moved his feet squelched in their sodden trainers.

He covered his face with his wet hands, as if to block out my gaze, as I suddenly realised where I had seen him before. On my way out of church last Friday afternoon after a funeral, I had been approached by him with a request for £1.60 – the bus fare for him to visit his dying grandfather in Stafford hospital.

'How's your grandad?' I asked, and when he didn't reply I opened the door. 'You'd better come inside.'

The young man stumbled into my study, sobbing out loud, and I was instinctively relieved when my husband also came in, through the back of the house.

'Oh Mark, this is . . .' I looked at our visitor, as he gritted his teeth, shaking now from head to foot as if frozen, even though steam was rising from him in

11

the dry heat of the study.

'John,' he moaned, clutching his abdomen in obvious pain. 'My name's John. *Can* you help me, please? I'm homeless and I can't stand sleeping out another night in this rain!'

As a parish priest, I have a policy never to give money to callers at the door. But food and dry clothes are another matter, and so we sat John down and while Mark made him a mug of tea and a sandwich I sat and listened to his story.

It was a very sad and simple one. His parents, who were both alcoholics, had kicked him out. They were, in fact, not his real parents, but adoptive ones who had always physically abused him. His grandfather was the only person he was close to, and he was now dying in hospital.

'For the past three nights I've been sleeping on the back stairs of the maisonettes on Chadsmoor,' John whispered, clutching his stomach again and rocking from side to side, 'but it's so wet and scary, and . . . and I'm really hungry!'

This being the case, I expected him to devour the food and drink that Mark had brought. But although he took the mug, and broke pieces off the cheese sandwich, he seemed too agitated to eat or drink. 'What am I going to do?' he repeated, staring through the thick spectacles at the torrential rain. He had never intended to become homeless, but he couldn't go back to his parents – he was scared of them. And soon there wouldn't even be his grandad to talk to.

As we talked, trying to calm him, he started to say that if he only had £10 he could stay with a friend of his for the weekend. This friend needed the money because he had a wife and baby to support.

Mark and I exchanged a look over our visitor's head. Drying out, he gave off an almost chemical smell and a clamminess that went beyond the wet weather. His blotchy face was now crimson, his eyes almost manic behind the flashing glasses.

I told him quickly about our policy never to give money, but suggested we make up a bag of groceries for him to take to his friend in lieu of the £10.

'If you're homeless, the council has an obligation to find you some accommodation,' Mark explained. 'I'll go with you to their offices on Monday, if it'll help.'

John nodded, teeth chattering, tears rolling down his cheeks into the fast cooling tea. 'That's really good of you, mister,' he said, 'but I still don't know how I'm going to get through the weekend. If you could just let me have £10, I'll bring it back when I get my Giro.' He looked at me apologetically. 'My mate won't take me in for grocery, see. He needs money too.'

Eventually, reluctantly, we agreed to 'loan' him the money and just for good measure gave him some bread and milk, tea bags and sugar and other basic necessities in a carrier bag.

Then, feeling a bit like an ageing mother sending her errant son off to school in the rain, I found a green kagoul from the cloakroom and helped him into it.

'Our son doesn't wear it now,' I explained, as I pulled the hood over his agitated head, 'and it'll stop you getting any more soaked on your way to your friend's.'

'Thank you, Vicar.' The strange young man hugged me tightly, and then formally shook hands with Mark. 'I'll be back on Monday morning to go to the council,' he promised, and I was glad to see that, although still clutching his stomach from time to time, he seemed to have lost his desperation. There was almost a purposeful look about him as he strode away from the vicarage back into the driving rain.

'I wonder if he *will* be back,' Mark mused, following me inside, 'or if that's the last we'll see of him.'

'Perhaps I should give that Ann a ring – see if she knows him,' I said, wishing I'd thought of it before.

Ann Peplow was a middle-aged woman we'd met a couple of weeks previously at a meeting of the Chadsmoor and District Residents' Group. An outspoken, down-to-earth Christian, she had spoken about Chadsmoor's underlying problems with drug and alcohol addiction, a problem I would never have suspected from my ageing and timidly diminishing congregation at St Chad's.

Dialling the number she had given me almost as an afterthought, I began to describe our distressed, homeless caller and what we had done to try and help him.

There was an embarrassed silence, and I began to realise just how naïve we had been in our dealings with John. 'Oh, Carol!' Ann finally sighed. 'That was "Specs"! He's a really bad heroin addict, and as for his having to sleep rough, it's all lies! He's got a lovely family. In fact his mother is nearly out of her mind with worry about him!'

She told me a little more about John's background, including the fact that he had gone to school with her own children. 'My friend and I have been getting together for nearly a year now to pray about the whole drugs situation,' she told me thoughtfully before she rang off. 'Perhaps this is God's way of saying you should join us!'

2

A Basketful of Prayers

'The prayer of the righteous is powerful and
effective.' (James 5:16)

Rather reluctantly I arranged to see Ann and her friend
Sheila the following Wednesday afternoon at the vicarage.
It was my first year as team vicar of St Chad's and my
efforts so far had been to try and build up the congregation. Frankly, I didn't see how praying about local
drug addiction would help.

On the Wednesday morning, I opened the front door to
bring in the milk and to my amazement found a scruffy
white saloon car parked in the shadow of the big old
church. Inside were four men wearing woolly hats and very
furtive expressions.

'Who the . . . ?' Automatically I locked the door as I
stepped back inside. St Chad's vicarage, though within
sight of the main road, was hidden behind the church. On
a dark winter's morning, with a tall man from the strange
car approaching the glass door, its privacy suddenly felt
like isolation.

The doorbell rang. I thanked God for my swiftly barking
dog, and, remembering instructions given to all new female
vicars, put the chain on the door before opening it.

'Yes?' I peered through the crack and caught sight of an
unshaven face. Beneath the black woolly hat, fingers
flicked a card in my direction.

'Police. Undercover unit,' he said in an almost pre-occupied way. 'We're keeping surveillance on the car park next door. Just go about your business as usual, Reverend.'

Over the next hour or so I tried to do just that, conducting the midweek communion service, having coffee with the tiny congregation, then getting ready for a crematorium funeral. It was difficult to ignore the parked car with its sinister-looking occupants, especially as they brought their surveillance gradually closer and closer.

'Do you mind if we go into the back garden?' a second officer requested, flashing another ID at me, and, finally, 'We'd get the best view from the church hall, Reverend. Could you let us in there?'

St Chad's church hall was a typical late-1960s extension with a flat roof and huge windows. Used for the struggling Sunday school and pensioners' weekly bingo and beetle drives, it was sadly in need of a refurbishment we could not afford.

As I led the four shifty-looking policemen inside, I couldn't help thinking it looked a suitable place for what they intended doing there. Three sets of plate glass windows faced the council car park opposite the Flaggin' Duck public house, their faded orange swirl-patterned curtains doing nothing to obscure the view.

Asked by the first officer if we had noticed any suspicious activity in the car park, I frowned. 'There does seem to be a lot of coming and going out here, especially at night,' I realised. 'Often when we're in bed, we hear brakes squealing and car doors slamming. And there's always someone hanging around outside the phone box.'

When Ann arrived with Sheila, she too mentioned the public telephone box on the edge of the car park. 'That's where most of them ring from to get their supplies,' she said, shaking her head as she sat down. 'Those who don't have access to a mobile phone, that is!'

Over coffee I described my hair-raising morning with the police, and Sheila nodded. 'They have a purge from time to time. It'll all be in the *Chase Telegraph* on Friday week if they manage to arrest anybody.'

'It's the big boys, the dealers, that they're really after,' Ann explained knowingly. Then, opening her shopping bag, she took out a small wicker basket and a plastic bag, which I saw held brightly coloured cardboard stars. Last, she took out a little wooden crucifix, which she stood on the coffee table.

'Each of these stars has the name of a heroin addict,' she explained, as she emptied them on the table before the cross. 'What we do each week is put them in the basket and offer them and their families to our Lord.'

'Let's do that first then,' I suggested quietly, as I cleared the coffee mugs away. Humbled, I felt moved by their own, Spirit-led initiative.

The three of us sat around the improvised altar, the pale afternoon sunlight suddenly cutting across the wintry day. A sense of peace in God's presence was tinged with a need and longing I couldn't identify. As we prayed, Ann sketched biographical details of each person named.

'This is Darren. He was in the army until the heroin got him . . . And Katie. She's an eighteen-year-old user who has been a prostitute since she was fifteen . . . Bryony's baby died last year. He was born with too much heroin in his bloodstream.

'I grew up in Chadsmoor, and went to school with most of the parents of these kids,' she explained when I commented on her in-depth knowledge. 'I know first hand the struggles they've had just accepting that their son or daughter is on hard drugs. The worst thing is knowing that once they're hooked, they'll do anything – rob, break into houses, sell their bodies – anything just to get the money for their next fix!'

'Yes, and because this is such a small community, everybody knows!' Sheila put in quietly. 'I know John's mum, for instance – the lad who came to you on Friday. She's so ashamed of him and the things he's done that she feels she can't face people any more.'

Ann nodded as she gently shook the name stars in the basket. 'Yes, because even at my church – I'm a Catholic – the attitude seems to be that you must be a pretty useless mother if your kids have turned to drugs.'

'Do you think John's mother would like to see me?' The words were out almost before I realised it.

As the two women looked at each other in obvious surprise, I blurted out, 'I-I mean, I don't have any *personal* experience of this, but . . .'

'You're like us,' Ann stated, nodding to the photograph of our grown-up daughter, son-in-law and two tall step-sons in pride of place on top of the television set. 'You may be a vicar, but you're a mother too. I'll tell Brenda that when I ask her to come. In Chadsmoor at the moment, we all need to be mothers against drugs!'

3

MAD or What?

'Come to me . . . and I will give you rest.'
(Mathew 11:28)

'Mothers against drugs.' The phrase stayed with me, even after Mark pointed out that its initials spelt 'MAD'.

'P'raps we are,' I reflected, only half joking. 'Mad to come here, instead of some leafy parish in Sussex!'

As the weeks went by I was discovering the extent of the drugs problem in this seemingly ordinary little place. As Sheila had predicted, there was a front page report in the weekly paper following my visit from the police. 'Heroin haul on Chadsmoor car park.' And it wasn't the only report. Every week there was at least one story in the local daily paper about drugs-related cases and crimes. Nine times out of ten the address of the defendant would be in my parish. It was also possible, just by walking through Chadsmoor, to come face to face with the thin, sinister-looking addicts I had somehow missed before. They lurked by the phone box and the newsagent's shop, or draped themselves on the ornamental wrought iron bench, kindly supplied by European funding and usually wreathed with discarded fish and chip wrappers. Banned from the shops because of their looks and reputations, they gave off an air of misery and neglect not easy to put into words.

Going around the parish, I heard more and more stories, all of them involving heroin. One day an old lady to whom

I took home communion showed me a photograph and asked me to pray for her grandson, a good-looking boy in a school blazer.

'He's not ill,' she confessed, waiting until her husband was out of the room. 'He's a drug addict. Tom's that upset he won't even let me mention it. But Jason promised me last week he was going to give it up. He asked me for £5 – for food – he swore it was for food – and when I give it him, he said, "I love you, Nan."'

As she reached for a tissue to wipe her eyes, I thought of the scene in the vicarage, when John had hugged me, relievedly expressing his thanks for the 'fix' we had unwittingly provided.

Next day I went to a women's fellowship meeting and heard a story about two elderly members being pestered in their bungalows by two young men who wanted to sell them a kettle and an iron for a couple of pounds.

'They said they needed the money for the electric meter,' one of them said meaningfully, 'but I know better than that!'

Several of the ladies nodded, and after she left the meeting, pulling her worn coat around her, one of them told me under her breath, 'Dot's daughter got in with one of them druggies and now he injects her with the stuff several times a day. They've got a little girl, nearly four. Dot worries herself sick about little Molly!'

This unappetising face of Chadsmoor had just not been in evidence when I came to be interviewed for the post of team vicar all those months ago. I realised, as I walked back to the vicarage, that it wasn't because anyone was deliberately trying to hide the facts. It was simply that our congregation, many of whom came by car from nearby Cannock, just had no inkling of the scope and depth of the problem.

As I walked past the well-known row of shops, greeting

people, I felt the indefinable, irresistible tug of the Holy
Spirit, reminding me that though he didn't need to, Jesus
had spent his time with outcasts and sinners. If he were in
Chadsmoor 'in the flesh' today, I had no doubt at all the
group of people he would be seeking. It might be safer, and
definitely more comfortable, to keep locking our church
door and closing our communal church eyes to the
village's heroin problem. But I already knew there was no
way I could do that and follow God's will in this place!

Over the next few Wednesday lunchtimes Ann, Sheila,
Mark and I prayed fervently that God would show us how
to help the local addicts and their families. We met in the
vicarage over a sandwich lunch, offering the names on the
stars Ann had brought along with her basket and crucifix
– names which up to that point I could not yet match with
faces. The congregation of St Chad's were as yet un-
involved, though Ann stressed the need for us to make it
known that the prayers were going on.

'You don't know how much it'll mean to some of the
families, particularly the mothers of the addicts, just to
know that the church is concerned,' she said.

Catching the hint of a shadow in her face, I said
nothing, but I was already beginning to realise from her
own vicarage prayers that Ann had more than an objective
interest in this particular social problem.

'Maybe you should advertise in the church magazine,'
Sheila suggested as we finished packing away our props,
now stored at the vicarage. 'Something like "We meet every
Wednesday at one, and we're MAD!"'

'Yes,' I agreed, happily scribbling the slogan into my
diary. 'You never know, it might even reach the ex-addict
we're hoping God will send!'

During our prayers it had come to us that what we really
needed was someone with 'hands-on' experience of drugs,
who had been healed of their addiction by the Holy Spirit.

But as I was fast discovering, Chadsmoor was not Hong Kong, and I was certainly no Jackie Pullinger with a wonderful ministry among the tough and the lost!

The notice went into both the bi-monthly magazine and the weekly notice sheets. But though I preached about Chadsmoor's hidden problem, and mentioned it conversationally to the congregation, it really did seem a taboo subject.

I could understand that, because my little district church, like many others, was struggling with an icy, impractical, hundred-year-old building, a diminishing congregation and a crippling parish share. Its rationale was merely to survive, bolstered up by the memories of the grand and glorious Christian ghosts of the past, whose increasingly dusty pews they had left unfilled behind them.

So no one came to the MAD prayers except the four of us. Then, unexpectedly, Ann turned up one evening at the vicarage with Brenda, whom she introduced as Specs's mum. A short, brown-haired woman in her late forties, she was obviously embarrassed.

'I felt I had to come and talk to you about that night John called on you,' she said, as I encouraged her to sit down. 'Ann's told me all the lies he told you and I just don't know where to put myself. That night, when he came home with the plastic mac and said he'd got me some groceries, I knew he must have conned somebody, but I never imagined it was you – that he'd come to the church!'

As the evening wore on, Brenda gradually told me John's story, beginning when he was a teenager and even the smell of cigarettes offended him.

'He used to keep on at me about it, because I smoke,' she said with a sigh. 'Then he left school and started going out with mates, and gradually into pubs, then clubs. He started smoking, then taking cannabis and the so-called designer drugs.'

Tears filled her eyes as she described how, as an older teenager, John seemed to have everything going for him. 'He got a job, he had a lovely girlfriend – everything was going his way. And then one of his so-called friends introduced him to heroin.'

'He told me about that, Brenda,' Ann put in quietly as she came in with the tea mugs. 'My son Danny and I met him one day on Chadsmoor, and he said they'd really conned him!'

'That might sound stupid to you, Vicar Carol,' Brenda said, as her sad eyes met mine. 'You might think all the kids have to do is say "no", like they tell them at school. But the pushers are people they grew up with and went to school with – not blokes in sunglasses and big cars, like on the telly. They believe them when they say it takes months to get addicted, or that you can give it up whenever you want!'

She broke off, fighting new tears as she remembered. 'I don't honestly think my John even knew he was a heroin addict until he got chicken pox!'

She described how, nursing her adult son through this children's complaint, she had realised that just when he should be improving he was growing infinitely worse.

'He had cramps and diarrhoea, shakes and sweats - a classic case of cold turkey, though of course neither his dad nor I recognised it,' she said. 'He had been too bad with the chicken pox to go out and get his fix, and that's what was making him so ill!'

Once started, she seemed relieved to be able to talk, and it all came out: the horror and shame of John's addiction, the terror that he would overdose, either accidentally or deliberately.

Finally, most poignantly, Brenda talked about the effect heroin had had on John's family. 'He's sold his dad's suits, my jewellery and his sister's clothes, which she'd worked so hard to buy and was really proud of. He's lied and cheated, threatened and mugged people for drug money. Twice he's been in court for shoplifting, and in a couple of weeks he's up again for breaching his probation order,' she reeled off unsteadily.

'He's been in detox, rehab and hospital. I'm fully expecting him to end up in prison now, and I'm so scared that would be the end of him!'

The three of us looked at each other, knowing there was no need to speak, even if we could find the words to say. Instead, in my nonplussed heart, I heard the words of Jesus saying gently and unmistakably: 'Come to me, all you who are weary and burdened, and I will give you rest' (Matthew 11:28).

'Let's pray,' I said, reaching for Ann's ready hand and Brenda's fearful fist. 'For John, when he goes to court, and for the Chadsmoor children growing up now, that they won't be fooled as easily as he was into thinking they can control this drug!'

4

Spreading the Word

'For there is nothing hidden, except to be disclosed.'
(Mark 4:22)

'I feel as if Chadsmoor is being woken up at last!' Sheila said at our next MAD meeting. We spent a long time in prayer, and in silence, waiting on the Lord, and when we had finished, another idea came, this time to Ann.

'I'm sure God is saying that we should get out Wednesday lunchtimes! If mothers can't get to us – are too ashamed or too sceptical – we should go to them. We should ask if we can speak at the women's meetings in the local churches.'

That day my contacts as vicar came in very useful, and I telephoned the leaders of the nearby Methodist and Baptist chapels to offer our talk, as well as arranging for us to visit St Chad's women's fellowship.

'Our prayer group is called Mothers Against Drugs,' Ann started, handing out cards Sheila's daughter had kindly printed on her computer. The verse we had been given for these outreach cards was from Jeremiah 31:16: 'Stop your crying and wipe away your tears. All you have done for your children will not go unrewarded. They will return from the enemy's land.'

'We know fathers suffer too, but we are speaking to mothers because as mothers you all need to know that there may come a time when your children will tell people

25

you are dead. They will look us in the eye and say that you hate them – that you have beaten them up and turned them out into the street. They will even say that they never had a mother. And that's because their "mother" is now heroin!'

Ann's eloquence brought silence, and then, as if given permission to speak, one after another of the Baptist church women began to describe their experiences, of fear of going out at night, of being accosted in their own homes during the day. And, most poignant of all, of the havoc caused in their own families by a youngster's, or even a middle-aged brother's or sister's, addiction to the hard drug.

'I can't come to the vicarage,' one youngish woman said as others around her nodded in agreement, 'but I'll certainly pray every week as you suggest!'

At Ann's request, we had given each member of our audience a small candle and also asked them to take a star out of the wicker basket and to pray for that particular person.

'It's Christian names only,' Sheila explained, as she later gathered the stars back into the basket, 'for the sake of confidentiality. But the Lord already knows who they are.'

The name I had picked up from the basket was 'John', so I prayed especially for Brenda's son, knowing that he was due in court that week. I remembered things his mother had shared with us the night she came to see me; how she always knew when he was injecting himself because he sang in the bathroom, while she listened in another room, crying silent agonised tears. I could well understand her greatest fear, that John would end up in prison, where drugs were rife and a young addict like him would be extra vulnerable to the demands, sexual and otherwise, of more hardened inmates.

There was, surprisingly, nothing in the *Chase Telegraph* that week about John's case. But the following Wednesday, when we met for our MAD prayers, Ann handed me a note. 'It's from Brenda,' she said with a wry smile. 'She said she had to write it down, otherwise she wouldn't be able to believe what's happened!'

Surprised, I opened the note and read that the week before, John had appeared at the court on charges of criminal damage, shoplifting and breach of probation. The magistrate, who had obviously seen him before, decided he should go to prison, and John was taken outside to wait for what was colloquially called 'the meat waggon'.

'They let him ring me on a mobile and he was crying, terrified out of his mind,' Brenda wrote. 'I was crying too, realising this really was the end. Prison would definitely finish him off! But then, as he stood there waiting for the van, a message came from the magistrate. He wanted him back in the court straightaway!'

As Sheila and Mark stared in surprise, Ann nodded, and I realised she already knew the end of the story.

'He, the magistrate, told John he'd changed his mind,' I read on. 'That he would give him one more chance – his very last! He was going to recommend that instead of sending John to prison, he be placed on probation for a further six months!'

'Apparently nobody could believe it,' Ann put in quietly, as I placed the note carefully before the crucifix on our homemade altar. 'He's never been known to reverse a decision before!'

'A miracle,' Sheila said excitedly, as Mark beamed his agreement. 'Isn't it marvellous, Ann?'

Seeing the shadow of wistfulness in Ann's blue eyes, I replied quickly for all of us, 'Well, at least an answer to one of our prayers!'

5

Secrets and Answered Prayers

'And a sword will pierce your own soul too.'
(Luke 2:35)

A week later I walked out of the vicarage and found a young policeman standing in the car park, talking to a group of youths. 'Reverend Hathorne? I'm Keith Sampson, your community policeman,' he said, as they moved away.

I stared, only just resisting the impulse to hug him. 'You know you're the answer to our prayers?'

He grinned, not at all fazed by my enthusiasm. 'I dunno about that. I understand you've written to the station as well?'

I had indeed written to the local police station a couple of weeks before to tell the police about our MAD group and its concerns about the Chadsmoor drugs problem, but had received only a 'your letter is receiving our attention' card in return. To actually have our own officer was more than we could have hoped for, and I couldn't wait to see Ann and Sheila to tell them the news.

'Keith has given us his card, with his pager, in case we need him urgently,' I reported at our next meeting. 'Meanwhile, he says he'll keep his eye on the place.'

'I suppose this is the equivalent of the bobby on the beat that the oldies are always bemoaning the loss of,' Sheila mused. 'The good old clip around the ear that used to send them home to get another one off their parents! Let's hope he gets to go into the schools as well.'

After Sheila had left to go back to work, Ann stayed on at the vicarage. Sensing her need to talk, I made some more coffee and we sat quietly until she said, 'Carol, I want to talk to you as a priest.' I nodded and Ann began, hesitantly at first, to explain about the anxiety I had perceived so often around her.

'My second husband, Alec, was a brilliant bloke, a straightforward family man. Even though he wasn't their real dad, he'd brought my three kids up and they adored him. Everything was fine for us all until two years ago, when he got cancer. Within eight weeks he'd gone from a healthy, fourteen-stone man to a skeleton. None of us could believe it when he died, and since then, well, if it weren't for my faith in Jesus, I couldn't survive . . .'

'And the kids?'

Ann sighed and shook her head. 'At first I thought they were OK,' she said. 'Emma got married young. Her husband already has a failed marriage and a couple of youngsters, but she's very down to earth and seems to be coping well. Lizzie's a bit of a dreamer, but basically she's a lovely girl who's always looking for stray dogs and lost causes. But it's Danny, the youngest, I'm really worried about, Carol. He really took it hard when Alec died – started going out to clubs, mixing with the wrong sort, and I found out a few months ago he's on heroin.'

Trying not to show my dismay, I sat and listened as she described her discovery that eighteen-year-old Danny was using the drug at one of the council flats on the small estate behind St Chad's.

'I haven't found out who lives there yet,' she said, drying her eyes, 'but I go round at night, while the kids are inside, and I sprinkle holy water from the stoop at my church and pray and pray. I don't care what happens, I've - I've got to save my son!'

No wonder Ann was so committed to the Mothers Against Drugs prayers, I realised, as I later joined Mark for our evening worship. She, more than any of us, had first-hand experience of what living with an addicted child really meant.

Next day, in the village, I encountered the little group of haggard, ashen-faced men and women who gathered round the phone box waiting for their fix. 'Mornin', Vicar,' one of them called experimentally, and I returned the greeting as normally as I could, though my heart was beating fast and I was very aware of the turned heads and staring eyes.

That evening I opened the church hall for the regular meeting of St Chad's District Church Council. With the fall in church membership the DCC had become rather sad, and I knew we would be lucky to get double figures. The discussion ranged as usual across the outstanding jobs that needed doing, both in the church and in the hall. It was decided, as it had been decided before, that a notice should be put up for people who were willing to tackle 'spring' cleaning, church lawn cutting and the like, to sign. My heart sank as I realised that even with my gentle cajolling, the list would flap, unsigned, until it finally fell down or someone replaced it with another unnoticed piece of paper.

Already the subject had been changed, and the cold air was full of grumbles about what was seen as unnecessary centralisation from the parish office in nearby Cannock, where funerals and weddings for St Chad's were now booked. We all sighed in a familiar way as our treasurer, Jane, presented the budget and drew our attention to the parish share, which we were unable to meet again.

'We'll just have to pray somebody wins the lottery,' quipped Fred Wilson, one of the churchwardens. 'Then we can settle all our debts, have the hall decorated and even get the heating fixed!'

'What – and stop being "God's frozen people"?' In spite of the joke I felt depression seeping into me as I later watched the little group disperse to the comfortable cars that would take them to the safety of their homes. I locked the door and turned to walk the few dozen yards to the vicarage, just as another car, old and red and very battered, screeched to a halt in the church car park. Automatically I drew back, realising I was alone and it was dark in the shadow of the looming old church. At the same time, a wiry figure jumped out of the car and hurried towards me.

'Vicar Carol?' the young man said, holding out his hand. 'I'm Peter Simms and I've been sent to talk to you. I'm a Christian, see, and I used to be a drug addict!'

* * *

'God really turned my life upside down,' Peter said, as we sat together with Mark round the kitchen table that evening. 'Before I met him I was into all kinds of designer drugs – cannabis, Ecstasy, speed – though not heroin. I lived in a kind of limbo.'

He went on to describe how he had come to faith through an old schoolfriend. 'Paul found me outside a club one night with a load of smackheads,' he said. 'I didn't even remember getting to his place, but he told me afterwards I had been on the brink of going off to the local shooting gallery . . .'

Mark and I exchanged a puzzled look and Peter grimly explained. 'There are places round here – usually squats or council flats – where people who are too nervous to inject themselves can always find somebody who'll shoot the needle into them for the price of a shot of the stuff themselves.'

I suppressed a shudder and Peter went on with his story. 'I didn't know it at the time, but Paul's a Christian and he prayed over me that night that Jesus would set me free and give me a new life, and the only way I can describe it is, well, the prayer was answered!'

Excitedly I told Peter how our own mothers' prayers about the local drug problem were also being answered. 'What we've felt all along is the need for someone who really knows what being addicted is like,' I said. 'Someone the young people will be able to relate to.'

'I just heard that you'd been to the women's group at my church. One of the ladies actually showed me your prayer card,' Peter grinned. 'And as the Lord has been putting it on my heart to pray for the users of Chadsmoor, I knew I had to come and find you.'

The following Wednesday our MAD prayers had a new dimension. Peter sat with Ann, Sheila, Mark and myself before the little crucifix, and as we placed the names on their star-shaped cards in the wicker basket, he prayed in tongues, with tears streaming down his face. Remembering how Jackie Pullinger described her Triad converts praying in tongues before many drug addicts were converted in the walled city of Hong Kong, I felt both awed and inspired by the presence of God in our small group.

I looked at Ann's pale and worried face. As we prayed for her son Danny and she told the others, through her own tears, about his heroin addiction, I suddenly knew that in Peter God had sent her someone who would be able to help her as probably no one else could.

'This thing is really evil. It's as if Chadsmoor is actually in the grip of Satan,' she whispered. 'He even stops the kids from getting food, because of course the shopkeepers won't serve them. They're afraid of being robbed, and rightly so.'

'The drug feeds them, or they think it does,' Peter

replied. 'The truth is, when heroin really gets you, you can't even face a hot drink in the morning until you've had your fix. The first step in trying to help Danny is to get him to the doctor and on a methadone programme, but obviously he's got to want to do it himself.'

'We must pray for that,' Sheila said. 'And for strength for Ann and the rest of the family.'

'I think we should pray too that the dealers who run these shooting galleries will be somehow removed,' Mark suggested. 'A kind of holy clean-up campaign!'

'The main one in Chadsmoor is Robbo Danks,' Peter told us. 'He's in a flat on the estate, and a steady stream of addicts go there to shoot up.'

As he described the location of the flat, it became clear that it was the same place Danny visited, and where Ann had been visiting late at night with her prayers and holy water.

'Danny's really worried in case I'm seen,' she said. 'If it's known his mother's a nosey parker in league with the church and the police, he says he'll get his legs broken. But I've told him I'd rather he had two broken legs than be dead from a heroin overdose!'

Before our MAD pray-ers disbanded that day, she turned to Peter, her face set in lines of desperation. 'Will you come with me tonight, Peter? I'm going to the flat again, and now I know Robbo's name I intend to go in and talk to him!'

6

Inside Information

'And you will know the truth, and the truth will make
you free.' (John 8:32)

'Street heroin is often cut with other substances to make it
go further – substances such as talcum powder, flour, brick
dust or even rat poison!' our speaker explained. 'That is
why overdose is so easy. For some users, their first use of
the pure stuff can, sadly, be their last!'

Trying not to feel conspicuous in my clerical collar, I sat
with a group of concerned parents and other school
governors at the drugs conference organised by the Local
Education Authority. During the coffee break it was good
to ask our speaker various questions, and I came away
from the event feeling that we in MAD were certainly not
alone in our concern for the Chadsmoor users and their
families.

'Drugline will supply speakers, and they also run a
needle exchange,' he said, scribbling down a phone
number. 'I think the Methodist church is also about to
start a kind of soup kitchen in Cannock. No matter who
they are, or how badly affected, addicts need food, just like
the rest of us.'

Remembering what Ann had said about the Chadsmoor
shops banning our local addicts, I heard a definite bell
start to ring! Meanwhile, the Lord seemed determined that
everything I touched in my ministry turned in a MAD

direction! A diocesan phone call came, asking if a trainee deacon, who was already a prison chaplain, might come and 'shadow' me one Wednesday.

'His name's Jim Blake, and he's hoping to be ordained at Petertide,' the Board of Ministry secretary explained. 'Basically he needs to learn what it's like being a vicar on a day-to-day basis.'

Jim was a lovely man, friendly and sincere, and he assisted me at the Eucharist and joined the little group of Wednesday communicants for coffee in the hall afterwards. When I told him the next item in the diary was Mothers Against Drugs prayers, he was obviously surprised. 'I didn't realise there was such a problem here,' he said. 'It's actually something I've had a lot of experience with, starting with the night my wife and I thought we were doing someone a good turn . . .'

He described how late one Bank Holiday Monday a few years before, he and his family were getting ready for bed when a banging came at the front door.

'It was really frantic, and because we live in a bit of a rough area near Wolverhampton, we were afraid somebody had been attacked and was coming to me for help, knowing I was a church worker. When I opened the door I found two girls, about eighteen years old. They looked terrible: exhausted, dirty and, frankly, scared stiff. I let them in, much to my wife's alarm, and they started crying and told me they had nowhere to spend the night. They were sisters, and the live-in boyfriend of the one had thrown them both out when the other came to Liverpool to stay with them.'

Remembering our experience with 'Specs' I nodded, and Jim went on to describe how he had sat them down and asked his wife to get them a drink and some food while he decided what to do with them. 'I wasn't about to hand over cash because I've been conned before,' he said. 'So I rang the nearest bed and breakfast place and was told there was a double room there they could have for £25. We had just about that amount in the house, so I got the car out and my wife and I drove them there. We booked them in, paid over the money, made sure they actually went to the room, and drove away thinking we'd done our good deed for that Bank Holiday and hoping that if one of our kids ever turned up destitute on a doorstep somebody would do the same for them.'

'And then?'

He caught my eye ruefully before continuing. 'Well, early next morning I thought I should ring the bed and breakfast to find out how they were. I had some altruistic idea that they might need help getting to a railway station or something. And lo and behold, the receptionist told me they weren't there. The minute we drove off the night before, they'd gone to the desk, asked for the money back, and disappeared into the night. They were obviously a couple of smackheads who really thought they'd won the lottery that night. And the hotel was glad to see the back of them!'

After our prayers, Jim shared with us some of the drug-related problems he came across in his prison chaplaincy. 'Since I've been there, I've tried to help a lot of addicts,' he said. 'My wife got used to them, and we've even had them to stay at the house following their release. The saddest thing I've ever seen is somebody dying from the long-term effects of cocaine, even though they no longer take it!'

He spoke about the availability of drugs in some prisons, brought in sometimes even in the clothes the inmates' babies wore when visiting (small babies being exempt from being searched). 'It's a case of dog eat dog,' he said sadly. 'And if you can do even one thing here in Chadsmoor to stop another addict from going inside, well, I'll be adding my MAD prayers to yours!'

Before Jim left that day he promised to send us the booklets used in prison to try and alert addicts to the dangers of sharing needles, as well as details of detox programmes. 'Though basically all you have to do with a heroin addict is to lock them in a room for about a week with no access to the substance,' he said quietly. 'Physically it's very unpleasant for them, but if they can do it, there is light at the end of the tunnel.'

'Specially if it's the light of Christ!' Peter rejoined, as he held Ann's hand tightly across the table.

We all said 'Amen!' to that!

7

A Warm Welcome

'For I was hungry and you gave me food.'
(Matthew 25:35)

'I wouldn't lie to a vicar now, would I?' The man called
Robbo Danks stared me straight in the eye and I felt the
hairs stand up on the back of my neck. Looking past the
tall, scruffy figure into the shady interior of the council
maisonette, I wondered why I had ever agreed to come on
this visit with Ann.

'I already told her!' Robbo went on, jerking a nicotine-
stained thumb in Ann's direction. 'I've never seen her lad
using drugs, and even if he did, he needn't come in here to
do it. There's plenty of other places!'

As he took a step towards us over the threshold, we
both instinctively stepped back. But frankly Robbo looked
too frail to harm us, his height accentuating the under-
nourished state of his body. His clothes were ill-fitting and
grubby; his thinning hair matted to his head.

'I don't want no trouble, Vicar,' he said through a
fit of coughing. 'But you, Ann, whatever your name is,
just stay away from my place with your mumbo jumbo!
An' tell that funny bloke – that Christian Peter – to do
the same!'

As the rickety door slammed in our faces, Ann and I
turned and made our way back to the main road. Opposite
Robbo's flat was a playground, looking bleak and bare in

the wintry weather. 'It makes my blood run cold to think that the kids playing here see the addicts in and out of Robbo's place,' Ann said. 'That's why I shall carry on with the prayers and the holy water, no matter how much he complains!'

'It sounds as if Peter's making his mark there too,' I reflected. 'And I know Mark's still praying for the evil influence to be removed. If it weren't for the sheer wickedness of what Robbo Danks is doing to the youth of our community I could almost feel sorry for him!'

As our regular prayers continued, we began to feel strengthened by God's grace. Gradually, new mothers joined us, including one from the Catholic church, whose son had been an addict for many years. 'I've been so ashamed,' Joan confessed with tears. 'My marriage broke up because of Terry's lying and stealing, and the only time we had any peace was when he was in prison. He's my only child and yet sometimes I feel I hate him!'

Another new member, Susan, put her arm around her. 'My husband won't even go for a pint in Chadsmoor any more because he feels everybody knows what our Tessa has turned into,' she said. 'He used to be really proud of her, when she went off to the High School in her uniform, and then did so well in her exams.'

Most of the newcomers were unchurched, though we did have an occasional Pentecostal supporter who joined Peter in praying in tongues over the names in the basket.

'We don't want to frighten them off, but at the same time we want them to feel that what we're doing is genuinely useful,' Mark pointed out one Wednesday. 'I'm beginning to think we should consider expanding – trying to help the actual addicts in a practical way, as well as spiritually supporting their families.'

Remembering my own ongoing concern that the addicts were not adequately fed, I kept thinking of Jesus encouraging the disciples to give the people something to eat by the sea of Galilee.

'Let's pray about the next step,' I suggested, 'and trust that God will tell us what it has to be.'

*   *   *

Less than a week later an advertising flyer appeared on the vicarage mat. 'Grand Opening of Warm Welcome,' it said. 'Mill Street Methodist Church, Cannock, offers food and friendship to anyone in need.'

The contact person, Marj Pearson, was someone Mark, Ann and I already knew from the housing coalition, and she was delighted when I suggested that a group from MAD should go along to see what 'Warm Welcome' was offering.

'We are getting some of the local drug addicts,' she said, 'though primarily the centre is for anyone – the elderly, the lonely, young mothers, anybody who needs a bit of practical support.'

Mill Street Methodist was very different from St Chad's in that the building was warm and modern, with a comfortable hall and well-equipped kitchen. As Ann, Peter, Mark and I walked in for the first time, Marj came from behind the counter to greet us. I looked around. There were small tables, bright with checkered cloths and flowers. On each table was a plate of bread, and the appetising smell of soup wafted from the kitchen.

The Methodist minister, the Revd Hardacre, sat near the stage, talking quietly to a man in a ragged overcoat, while dotted around at the far tables were stark, emaciated figures I recognised almost instinctively now as heroin users. One man, tattooed on his face and neck, talked animatedly to a group, raising his arms for emphasis, while others sat motionless, barely lifting their eyes. Nearer to the kitchen hatch sat two elderly women, their shopping bags at their splayed feet, and tea and sandwiches in front of them. The entrance to the church led directly off the hall, unobtrusive yet available, and in the background, soothing music played.

Marj and her friend Ellen joined us as we pushed two tables together then collected some food. 'We charge fifty pence if people can afford it,' Ellen explained, as I put a donation in the tin, 'but mainly we want our customers to know this is available, even if they're penniless.'

A small queue was beginning to form at the counter as people received not only simple food, but a kind word and an encouraging smile from the two middle-aged women who served them.

This was surely Christianity in action, I thought. Mother figures doing what mothers were renowned for doing the world over: offering food and comfort in the face of hardship and temptation. If only we at St Chad's could provide something similar for the heroin addicts of Chadsmoor!

8

'He's My Brother!'

'Bear one another's burdens.'
(Galatians 6:2)

There were several obstacles in our way. First, unlike the
Methodists' Warm Welcome, St Chad's church hall was
cold, neglected and decidedly unwelcoming. Second, as a
group, Mothers Against Drugs did not have a single penny
in resources. Last, but definitely not least, I couldn't
imagine, even in my wildest dreams, the church council
agreeing to any scheme that invited heroin addicts through
our doors!

God already knew the obstacles, but we told him about
them anyway, using our MAD time to pray for the
miracles we knew were so badly needed if life were ever to
change for the young people named in our prayer basket.
There was often news of them through the grapevine, most
of it depressing. 'Specs' had been beaten up in
Wolverhampton for begging on someone else's patch; Matt
and Darren, who spent time and money at Robbo's flat,
had been arrested for shoplifting in Somerfield; Ann's
Danny was now on a methadone programme and making
life difficult for everyone. But everything seemed to come
to a head that particular Monday morning with a call from
our local undertaker.

'Carol?' Bob said, an urgency in his voice I hadn't heard
before. 'I've just sent a family along to see you. Their

twenty-seven-year-old son was found dead on Saturday from a drugs overdose. They'd like you to take the service at St Chad's, please.'

The doorbell rang almost before I had put the telephone down. A moment later, I showed Mary Bennett and her sister Alice into the lounge. They were two Chadsmoor women I vaguely knew by sight, and they had barely nodded a greeting before Mary, a pale, pretty woman in her forties, began emitting the almost incoherent litany of what had happened to her son Wayne.

'He-he told me he didn't use it no more! He and his brother Matt had just got a council flat over at Rudgeley and they seemed to be doing well – really well! But then Saturday night . . .'

As she broke down, her sister took up the story of how Matt, having left Wayne in the flat, went back on Saturday evening and found him dead on the floor. 'Matt's not . . .' Alice glanced at her sister awkwardly. 'He-he's not p'raps as quick on the uptake as he could be. He always relied on Wayne, see.'

'All their lives they've stuck together – the-the Mitchell brothers their mates called 'em, cos of their haircuts!' Mary whispered.

Picking up my notebook, I started to gently ask questions about Wayne. It was a pitifully short biography. The eldest of four children; attended Chadsmoor infants and juniors, and Blakemore High; worked for a while in a toy factory; liked to go out for a good time at the local pubs and night clubs.

The funeral took place a week later on a gentle spring morning when the crocuses were in bloom. As his mother keened and moaned, unable to be comforted, Wayne's coffin was carried down the aisle by six equally distraught bearers, including Matt, cousins and friends, and a very stitched-up Specs. From the back of the church, gloomy even on this lovely day, poured the strains of, 'He ain't heavy – he's my brother!' from the tape player.

The addicts were out in force – thin, hollow-eyed, driven men and women who had once been the youth of our community. They had shared Wayne's childhood and growing years, and somewhere along the line, at night club, street corner or on somebody's living room floor, they had learned to share his addiction too.

Surprising people were there. The ex-serviceman called Dennis, who worked hard for the local British Legion, confessing before the service that Wayne had lived at his house for several months last year, and that his own son Tony was a heroin user too. At the back, silent and tight-lipped, stood Fred, my churchwarden, covering a funeral duty for the verger, who had gone down with flu. It was hard to ascertain just what Fred was thinking as the swaying, desolate procession went down the aisle, but I knew how alien it must all seem.

Not so surprising, in an unobtrusive side pew, stood Ann, Peter and Sheila, the members of MAD who knew just how much their prayers were needed today. I silently thanked God for the support their presence gave to me as well as to Wayne's mother.

As the music ended, the addicts stared hauntedly at nothing while I said the opening prayers, the moaning of Mary punctuating every phrase. They shuffled and stood up stiffly in the main body of the church for the first hymn, with earrings, tattoos and ashen faces set against spiky peroxide hair – the girls in skintight lycra trousers and skimpy white tops barely covering pierced belly buttons.

Faces blotched, the young male bearers in their white shirts seemed oblivious to the hymn books in their hands. There was an atmosphere of deep malcontent, and I remembered the story I'd once heard, that heroin addicts, like vampires, fear the cross of Jesus Christ.

The hymn, 'The Lord's My Shepherd', ended and I read from Romans about nothing separating us from the love of Christ. It had been hard to choose a reading, but this one seemed to fit. It was unequivocal about the horrors we can and do face, and the glory that can also be at hand.

'Good job the drugs squad didn't pop in,' Bob the undertaker said as we later set out for the cemetery in the flower-laden hearse. 'They'd have had a field day in St Chad's today!' I soon found out that his levity masked a fierce anger at the waste of Wayne's life. 'When we got him into the chapel of rest, we were all brought up short,' he said, shaking his grey head. 'Such a perfect young body. Apart from the obvious, there wasn't a mark on him!'

I nodded, staring out to where shocked and broken spectres were gathering around the still figure of Mary as she was almost lifted into the limousine. I wondered how on earth she would survive the ordeal of the graveside.

'Still,' Bob said, as he expertly put the hearse into gear. 'I knew as soon as I heard about it you'd be the right vicar. And as we've seen from the turn out, it was certainly the right church!'

9

Stepping Out in Faith

'Now faith is the assurance of things hoped for.'
(Hebrews 11:1)

'Item four on the agenda,' I announced at the next church
council meeting. 'Plans for a Wednesday drop-in centre
here in the church hall.'

As the small semicircle of faces turned in my direction, I
took a deep breath and began to describe how, through the
Mothers Against Drugs prayers and Wayne Bennett's
funeral, I'd felt the Lord prodding St Chad's into doing
something for the most vulnerable members of the local
community.

'It seems to me to be all about signals,' I explained,
hardly able to control the note of desperation that rose in
my voice. 'Every Wednesday morning now, there's the
midweek communion followed by coffee for the faithful
few who come along. Then the church and the hall are
firmly locked and everyone goes home. What sort of signal
does that give, not only to the drug addicts but to the
lonely, sick or bereaved – anyone in fact in need of Jesus'
love here in Chadsmoor?'

'Well, the church has been accused of being a clique,'
said Derek Wallis, our deputy churchwarden breaking the
very pregnant silence, while at the side of me Fred Wilson
put in, surprisingly: 'And we are supposed to be reaching
out to people, bringing them in . . .'

'Not locking them out, certainly!' agreed Jane Jackman, our treasurer. 'My main concern, Carol, as you might expect, is how you are going to pay for this new venture. You know what our financial situation is like!'

As grim nods and negative murmurs started to spread like cold germs, I took another deep breath, and with an inspiration that came straight from the Lord said, 'We've also stopped giving to any missionary causes, Jane. That can't be right! In my experience if we take a chance and genuinely step out in faith and generosity, and with lots of prayer, God will give us what we need and more.'

Almost without realising I was doing it, I began to recount the encouraging true story of the new Sunday school that had been started, against all odds, in my last parish, where I had served as an assistant curate. 'There had been no Sunday school at St Mark's for about twelve years, and every church event and formal meeting ended with someone saying wistfully, "If only we could get some youngsters into the church again!" My own experience, growing up in the fifties, was that in a place like that, Sunday school worked best in the afternoon, when Mum and Dad were having a snooze. So at the next PCC meeting I asked for volunteers to help me run a Sunday afternoon group for local youngsters. The volunteers then got together to plan – and, more important, to pray – and a few weeks later a luminous green poster went up outside St Mark's, which said: "Grand opening of new Sunday school. All welcome!"'

'And did anyone come?' Beryl Arnold, who took care of our dwindling electoral roll, looked at me wide-eyed, and I felt the atmosphere in the dingy hall quicken as I exclaimed, 'Yes! We were thrilled to bits because that first Sunday afternoon we got twenty-five children, most of whom are still around and were actually confirmed last year in Worcester Cathedral! But the real reason I'm telling you this story is that about a month after I broached the subject of a new Sunday school, I found out from the church treasurer that in recent weeks a legacy had come into St Mark's through a solicitor acting on behalf of a woman who had grown up there decades before. The terms of the legacy were that it could only be used for a Sunday school. The interest alone means the kids have the most amazing sound system, staging for drama productions and outings to the pantomime every year!'

'So we *could* get the richest drop-in centre in the world?' warden Fred put in, without humour. From his position beside me at the table, he looked around at the council members, most of whom he had known all their lives. He sighed. 'As you can see, friends, the vicar is rather enthusiastic about this venture, and I do feel we should take on board the fact that we have done very little about outreach here at St Chad's in recent years. But we shouldn't be tempted to forget that we also have a responsibility to our present congregation. The last thing we want is to put them in any danger, or make them afraid to come in case they are attacked or robbed by addicts we are harbouring around the church hall. I should, therefore, like to formally propose a compromise – that the so-called Wednesday drop-in should be adopted for a trial period of six months, and then the position brought back to the church council to be reviewed!'

'Proposal seconded!' I caught Mark's eye and his consoling grin as he held up his hand. It was a compromise, and we'd talk about it later. Meanwhile, the unease that had seeped almost insidiously into the gathering during Fred's speech disappeared again, as if by magic!

Hardly daring to breathe, I put it to the vote: 'All those in favour. A Wednesday drop-in centre starting as soon as possible for a trial period of six months.'

At my other side the church secretary, Margaret,

expressed something of my own surprise, and none of my delight, as the hands went into the air. 'Carried unanimously,' she said.

*   *   *

The next few weeks were busy ones. I carried out my usual parish duties with the added impetus that the date for the grand opening of the Wednesday drop-in had been prayerfully set for the week after Easter, the second Wednesday in April. An announcement was placed in the St Chad's bi-monthly newsletter *Chat*, as well as on the weekly pew sheets, and I tried, without alarming the congregation, to prepare them for the new project in words from the pulpit. Sadly, I had grown used to receiving no response to sermons – a situation which, coming from a more affirming church, had always had the power to perplex and hurt me. So it was with delight as well as surprise that I found Maureen and Claudia, two of our more active church members, waiting for me after one Sunday morning when the air in St Chad's had been particularly icy and I'd felt, despite all my preparatory prayers, that I was banging my head against a frozen, solid wall.

'Claudia and I have been talking, Carol,' Maureen began, as we moved to a corner of the draughty portico after everyone had left. 'We should like to come along and help with this new coffee morning you're starting after Easter. I'd like to bring Ted too if that's OK.'

I bit my lip. Maureen was a relatively new member of St Chad's, whose husband had suffered a stroke the year before. It was to her credit that she was always trying to involve him in those church activities he could manage.

'That's great, Maureen,' I said, as my eyes met those of the older lady, Claudia. 'You're both an answer to prayer, but I should explain that the drop-in isn't going to be a coffee morning as we know it. It's more a place of safety, and kind of fellowship . . .'

'. . . for the local druggies,' Claudia finished. She nodded her warmly hatted head, and I remembered how moved I had been by a very fine poem she had written in a recent St Chad's *Chat*. A poem about a prisoner waiting to be shot at the first light of dawn.

'I'd still like to come,' she went on, as Maureen, after a moment's thought, nodded in agreement. 'After all, it's true what you said in your sermon. What we do for the least of people, we do for him!'

As one, we all looked up at the beautiful elaborate crucifixion scene – the huge wooden rood, dramatically suspended over the entrance to St Chad's dark chancel as a tribute to the faithful fallen of the First World War. A lump came into my throat as I remembered how, on my very first visit here with Mark, the figure of Jesus between his mother and the beloved disciple John had drawn my gaze and transfixed my heart, making me realise that despite the freezing building and the tiny, rather dour, congregation this was definitely where God was calling me to serve right now. Thanking Maureen and Claudia, I quickly locked up and hurried home to tell Mark about them.

'It's great that they're both from the congregation, because St Chad's needs to be involved,' I said, as we went about our preparations for lunch. 'When you think about it, we've got quite a mixture of denominations already among the MAD lot who'll be helping out. There's Ann with her holy water from the Catholic church, Peter from the Baptists . . .'

'And me about to become an Anglican curate!' my

husband reminded me. Our eyes met and we laughed, amazed and delighted as usual as we pondered the mysterious ways of our wonderful God. For he had been leading American-born Mark very clearly over the past few years – away from his longstanding work in the Methodist Church and towards some so far unrevealed future ministry in the Church of England.

'Anyway,' I said, as I set our plates on the kitchen table, 'now God's sending the volunteers, all we need is a nice bright poster like we had at St Mark's, a bit of funding, and a lot of faith!'

10

All Welcome!

'The knowledge of the glory of God in the face of
Jesus Christ.' (2 Corinthians 4:6)

'Wednesday drop-in: 11 am–2 pm!' the poster announced.
It was in flourescent orange, and the black letters were
several inches tall. 'ALL WELCOME!'

Underneath was a picture of a cup and saucer, the
inspiration of Steve, the signwriter from Hednesford,
letting passers-by know about the simple hospitality we
were offering.

'Wow!' Ann exclaimed, when I proudly unrolled it on
the floor at our next MAD prayers. 'That'll definitely
knock their eyeballs out!'

'I can't wait to put it on the noticeboard,' I said, 'but in
the meantime we've got loads of new things to pray for!'

Into our basket of stars that week went a plea for some
practical support, in financial as well as human terms. We
needed donations of basics such as tea, coffee and maybe
soup and bread, or the money to buy them. We needed
more volunteers to take care of the practical work as well
as to befriend the people we were so hoping would 'just
drop in'. More than anything else, we needed the support
of a prayerful covering to protect everyone involved in this
risky exposure to the insidious presence of heroin, peddled
so openly on the streets beyond St Chad's church doors.

The prayers continued – daily in the vicarage, weekly in

the group – and became the focus for my Lent sermons, based, as I had known from Ash Wednesday that they should be this year, on the face of Jesus Christ. On Mothering Sunday, when the congregation had swelled to thirty thanks to the visiting Brownies, I held up a perfect stately daffodil.

'In this flower,' I said, thanking God for once for St Chad's anti-wilt temperature, 'I can see the face of Jesus Christ, glorious in creation, there with his Father before this world was even created!'

Warming to my theme, I expanded on it, quoting from St Paul's first letter to the Ephesians, and the picture of God's plan for humankind, which I have always found personally inspiring. I was scarcely aware of the strange face in the congregation until, led by the Brownies, people began to come up to collect their traditional Mothering Sunday flowers to take home. Then, to my surprise, I recognised Marj Pearson from the 'Warm Welcome' in Cannock.

'I just felt called to come to your service today, Carol,' she later explained at the church door. 'And now I've seen your pew sheets and listened to your prayers about the Wednesday drop-in, I know why!'

My enthusiasm bubbling over, I told her how the Lord had brought our plans into focus after the MAD group's visit to the 'Welcome' soup kitchen, and made us realise they were his plans for this place too. 'We're just trusting him now to help us get it all together,' I said. 'We need money, of course, and helpers and oh lots of things!'

'You'll get them, love!' Marj gave me a hug. She took the amazing daffodil I instinctively offered and held it to her as she waved from the car park.

A couple of days later, as I was getting ready for a funeral, the telephone rang. It was Marj with the wonderful news that after an emergency meeting of the 'Warm

Welcome' organising committee, St Chad's Wednesday drop-in was to be given a donation!

'It's only £50, but it'll get you started,' Marj said, as I expressed my delighted thanks. 'And once people see things happening there, who knows what'll happen?'

Grateful as I was for the donation, I knew what I wanted to happen! Locking up the church hall after the pensioners' bingo session that week, I closed my eyes and imagined the place with gleaming newly painted walls and fresh bright curtains! The kitchen was outmoded and grubby. It had unaccceptable cluttered work surfaces, filthy windows with a row of mouldy milk bottles on the ledges, an open waste bin and a leaking water heater, which had made a rotting puddle on the grey lino by the sink. I knew without even making enquiries that the Health and Safety people would condemn the kitchen as unsuitable for the preparation of food and drink. As for the hall itself, the walls were grimy and the hard wood floor held generations of dust, its tendrils clinging behind every moveable electric heater and wooden stacking chair. Neglect and apathy hung in the air like a sickness of the spirit waiting to settle on whoever had the misfortune to wander into the place.

But what could our elderly congregation do? Those who hadn't had hip replacements had suffered varyingly from recent heart attacks or bereavements that seemed to have knocked all the stuffing out of them. Their painting, decorating and floor scrubbing days were definitely over, no matter how many 'working parties' the DCC tried to organise!

Sighing, I walked to the dusty window, gloomy in the evening light. I gingerly picked up the edge of the stiff, cobweb-encrusted curtain with its orange swirls so reminiscent of the sixties. 'Oh Lord!' I prayed silently but fervently. 'HELP!'

'The Lord helps those who help themselves' is a cliché

that in this instance turned out to be true. In the close community of Chadsmoor, in shops, houses, schools and in street corner conversations, I let it generally be known that I was dismayed about the grisly state of the church hall, and that St Chad's itself was financially bankrupt. Even more significant was the fact that we no longer had able-bodied volunteers to undertake the sort of work that was needed before we could open up to the public. Within days, to my utter amazement, people appeared with exactly the skills and experience, the time and energy, that we needed!

'I know we only come to church at Christmas,' said Anthea from round the corner, whose father's and mother's funerals I had done within the previous year, 'but my Brian's retired from work now, and he was a painter and decorator. He'll be pleased to come and wallop the walls for you with stuff we've got in the garage!'

'First it'll all need scrubbing though, Carol,' Anthea's cousin Mary put in. Though far from young, and no longer a regular attender, Mary had tremendous energy and was always the first to be called on when St Chad's social committee planned its annual fund-raising Christmas and Springtime fayres.

Now she rolled up her sleeves and surveyed the dirty walls. 'It amazes me how folk can spend all their time and money sprucing up their houses, and yet they let God's house go to rack and ruin!' she said bluntly. 'Why, my old man's garden shed's in better nick than this place!

'Don't you worry, my love,' she finished, as Anthea nodded at her side. 'You won't know this hall by the time the girls have finished with it!'

'We have to thank God for all that's happening,' I said at the next MAD prayers. 'It's almost as if people outside the church are grateful for the opportunity to get involved. It is, after all, still their church, even though they don't come very often. Mary's sister Doreen is actually measuring up for new church hall curtains and offering to pay for them in memory of their mum, who apparently came here years ago!'

'Christianity in action, I think it's called,' Mark said as Peter and Ann grinned and nodded. 'And I think we'll get even more of it if you use all these offers as a basis for your intercessions on Sunday!'

I agreed, and in the prayers at the Eucharist that week thanked God for all the help we had been promised, thus making the official opening of our Wednesday drop-in possible in a month's time.

As I finished the prayers and turned to announce the next hymn, I saw the looks of surprise and almost unwitting interest among the members of the scattered congregation, though I could tell from their faces that not all were pleased at what I knew would be seen as interference from outsiders. After the service Joan and Ivan, a couple in their fifties, who before my time had been involved with the now defunct youth club, hung back to speak to me.

'If there's anything we can do to get the hall spruced up, Carol, just let us know,' Ivan said. 'We've been very lucky with our two girls. Neither of them have ever been involved in drugs, but we do see a lot on the estate where we live.'

'Yes,' Joan said, a little awkwardly, making sure she was out of earshot of the churchwardens. 'I like things nice; in fact I'm often accused of being house proud at home. It's worried me for ages that this place is such a mess!'

Over the next couple of weeks the transformation was complete. Brian and Ivan borrowed equipment, and stripped, sanded and polished the floor. Mary, Anthea and a little band of other ladies from the local estate got together with buckets of hot water, disinfectant and lots of elbow grease. Standing on tables, they tackled the grime-splattered walls and ceilings, first in the kitchen and then in the hall itself.

Finally, exhilaratingly, there was a smell of fresh paint as our volunteer decorator put up his scaffolding and climbed his ladders and refused downright all offers of payment for either his work or his materials. 'This cream paint's been cluttering up my garage for years, Vicar!' he grinned. 'I'm glad to see the back of it, to tell you the truth. As for my time, well, I'd only be wasting it in the old Duck!'

*   *   *

'The curtains! It's the curtains that make it a miracle for me!' I exclaimed blissfully to Mark the Tuesday before the drop-in officially opened. At each window hung heavy floral drapes, all beautifully lined with deep green cotton fabric that could be seen from the main road. Gone were the cobweb-coated orange swirls which, at the mere sight of hot water, would have disintegrated! They had been consigned (by me personally) to the church's usually empty wheely bin.

Instead of looking sad and neglected, St Chad's church hall was now bright and inviting, inside and out. Mark and I had earlier pasted up the dayglo poster on the roadside noticeboard. All we needed now were the people, and that, like everything else, was a matter for prayer!

11
Drop-in and Drop-outs

'I have come to call not the righteous but sinners to repentance.' (Luke 5:32)

The £50 donation from 'Warm Welcome' arrived on the day we opened. But though I was pleased, I was much too nervous to appreciate the significance of that 'holy coincidence' until later. With Mark, Ann and Peter, I helped set out tables and decorate them with pretty cloths and small vases of silk flowers we had scavenged from our various homes. Feeling very decadent, we plugged in all the newly cleaned electric heaters and filled three kettles. Worship music drifted from my CD player as we joined hands around the man-sized standing cross I had brought in from the vicarage, and prayed that all our hard work was not to be in vain.

'People need to know they can trust us,' Ann said wisely, as we settled down with mugs of coffee. 'That we're not connected with the police, or the social services.'

'Yes, it takes a lot of courage just to step over a church threshold. I know that from my own experience,' Peter replied. 'But once word gets round that we're here, and everybody really is welcome, then I think we'll have the place full.'

My colleagues had already agreed to pass on the word about the drop-in on the estate where Robbo Danks lived, and I knew both had other contacts in the drug world through Ann's son Danny, and Peter's old friends. But I still felt nervous, uncertain about what we had started, and inadequate about my own ability to cope should the church hall suddenly fill up with heroin dealers and users.

I needn't have worried, because on opening day our clientele consisted of one young woman, confirmed the previous year into our ageing congregation, who brought her two-year-old twins and her mother. Between us we filled two tables, drank soup and ate beans on toast.

'Don't be disappointed at the small numbers, Carol. The atmosphere is wonderful!' Alison assured me with a hug, before she left. 'I shouldn't say it, but it's become quite an effort coming to church on Sundays. I don't often go away uplifted at all, and it's so cold people never stay behind to talk, let alone share their faith. But here, I dunno, it just feels as if there's hope.'

'Hope is what the gospel is all about, after all,' Mark said quietly, as we later began to pack away our things to be stored in the vicarage until the following Wednesday. It came round alarmingly quickly and followed the same pattern as the previous week, with Fred and the half-dozen communicants from the midweek communion scurrying out after their coffee just as Ann and the other helpers arrived.

'Come on,' Fred said bluntly, 'before the vicar's drop-outs drop in!'

I followed, wanting to reassure them and invite them to break the habits of a lifetime and stay on for another cup of coffee. But just as Fred led several of the ladies towards his waiting car, a shout came from by the telephone box: 'Excuse me. Can you help this man, Vicar?'

The woman who called was hanging on to a tall, willowy individual who seemed in real danger of falling over. With the slam of Fred's car doors still ringing in my ears, I walked the few yards to the phone box. The man was sobbing and mumbling incoherently, stumbling against the woman as he gravitated towards the dirty glass walls. I had never seen anyone quite so blind drunk in my life!

'I'm scared he'll get run over,' the woman said. 'I was going to ring the police, but then I saw your sign and thought you might be able to look after him.'

Just then, right on cue, Ann and Deanna, her friend from another local church, came round the corner. 'Let's take him inside, Carol,' Ann said, as we somehow unwound him from the relieved woman and propped him up between the three of us. 'We'll get some black coffee down him.'

For the next hour the Wednesday drop-in played host to its first real client, Steve, whose addiction to alcohol was just as deadly and destructive as any of the heroin addictions we were to encounter later. His face raw from weeping, he continued to cry, sitting at the table near the heater, picking at his sore hands with their bitten nails, staring into space. All the time he talked a rambling gibberish that even he didn't seem to understand.

'Coffee for all of you!' Deanna placed three steaming mugs on the table in front of us, and Ann and I tried to get Steve to drink some. By the time he could stand unassisted, Ann had managed to find out that he was the father of a young addict who had been involved in a hit and run accident on Cannock Chase the year before. His marriage had broken up following his son's death, and he now lived alone in a council flat, haunted by memories and tormented by his daily need for vast quantities of cheap cider and lager. As the gentle praise music drifted across from the CD player, I noticed Steve's head turning in that direction. He frowned, looking puzzled, and I reached out and took his clammy hand.

'They're singing about Jesus, Steve,' I explained as my own heart responded to the uplifting sound. 'He's the one who can help you, if you'll only let him.'

For a split second Steve's anguished eyes met mine, and my held breath became a prayer. Then, almost savagely, he snatched his hand away and jumped to his feet, sending splashes of his third black coffee across the table cloth. 'Got to go!' he shouted. 'Got to get out!'

'He looks as if he should see a doctor,' Mark said, as we watched him weaving his way towards the door. 'Maybe we could persuade him . . .'

One of the advantages of living at St Chad's vicarage was that the doctor's surgery was only a hundred yards away. But it was obvious as Mark tried to intercept him that Steve had only one destination in mind. 'Going to the Spar!' he announced, as his thin unsteady figure went along the corridor. 'Going to the Spar!'

'Let's hope they won't serve him with any more booze!' Ann said under her breath. 'Come again, Steve!' she called. 'And remember – Jesus loves you!'

In the silence that followed, we all looked at each other. 'Oh dear,' I said. 'Somehow I don't think we handled that very well!'

'I know what you mean,' Deanna said thoughtfully as we gathered again around our standing cross. 'We were all so eager to help him he probably felt totally overwhelmed!'

A corner of Peter's mouth began to twitch into a smile. 'God's got a good sense of humour, as we all know really well,' he said, amid nods of agreement. 'While Steve was here I kept getting pictures of Ann trying to drag somebody in off the streets, and this poor bloke saying, "No, really, I don't want a cup of coffee and a chat! I'm actually on my way to work!"'

As a burst of delighted laughter rose among us, the door opened and Claudia and Maureen, our would-be helpers from St Chad's, came in. 'What a lovely sight – all hands joined around the cross!' Claudia exclaimed.

As they came to join us Maureen whispered, 'I haven't brought Ted. I thought, well, I'd see what it was like first.'

Curiosity brought several people through the doors during the next hour or so, including our little groups of decorators and cleaners, keeping Claudia and Maureen busy in the kitchen. Maureen had generously baked savoury scones the night before, and we were able to offer these with the lunchtime drinks.

'We'd like to pay, please, Carol.' An elderly couple from Chadsmoor Methodists paused before they left, the man holding out a pound coin. 'You can't provide all this for nothing!'

'I've been thinking about that too!' Quick as a flash, Deanna produced a collecting tin from her shopping bag. Across it she had pasted a label: Wednesday drop-in. 'I think we should keep this on the counter for those who can afford to pay a nominal sum,' she suggested, as the pound coin was cheerfully deposited into it. 'We *are* trusting God to provide for this venture, but at the same time people shouldn't be discouraged from giving if they can!'

'So long as the addicts don't think they *have* to pay,' Ann put in quickly as Deanna stood the tin in place. 'That would be enough to put them off, and we're not aiming to make a profit, don't forget!'

'No, but we could do with some proper organisation,' I said, pulling up a chair to join her. 'So as we're all together and things are pretty quiet, let's hold our MAD prayers and let's also talk about one or two practical matters!'

'You should really have elected a treasurer and all that before you started this thing, you know, Cazza,' Mark teased as we made our way back to the vicarage, laden with what seemed to be growing drop-in equipment in two large cardboard boxes. We paused and grinned ruefully at each other as we recalled the past hour of heated discussions between the many strong personalities in the leadership group God had given us for this venture. Already we could both see the threat of conflict between Ann and Peter (who were, heart and soul, for the provision of support for the heroin addicts), and the less-driven Christians like Maureen, whose agenda was also very personal. Deanna, meanwhile, just wanted to be of practical help, hence her election as our treasurer.

'I don't know about you,' I said firmly, as I lowered my box and unlocked the door, 'but I could do with putting my feet up for half an hour. I'm due to take communion to the nursing home at half-past four.'

At precisely 3.45 the doorbell rang. To my surprise I found the diminutive figure of Larry, a red-haired ten-year-old who spasmodically attended St Chad's Sunday school. 'Hello, Vicar Carol!' he beamed as he stepped off his bike. 'I'm here!'

'Yes. I, er, can see that, Larry,' I said, as his expression grew more expectant. 'Er, come in for a minute.'

Larry followed me into the lounge as I explained I was on my way out. He smiled and sat on the edge of a chair, patted the dog and accepted a glass of juice and some biscuits. Five minutes later he got to his feet, saying he had to go now. 'But I'll come again another week,' he promised, as Mark and I exchanged amused but rather dumbfounded glances over his auburn head.

'I wonder why he came?' I mused, as he got back on his bike and rode away, waving his hand at the end of the church building. A few minutes later, as I passed the dayglo notice again on my way to my next appointment, it all made sense. And a bubble of warmth and joy suddenly made the whole very mixed day worthwhile.

It was Wednesday. So Larry, bless him, had been doing his own bit of 'dropping in'!

12

A Circle of Prayer

'Give thanks in all circumstances.'
(1 Thessalonians 5:18)

Over the next few weeks we gradually built up a regular clientele, drawn through word of mouth and the wayside pulpit of our noticeboard.

There was Steve, the alcoholic, thankfully not put off by the over-enthusiastic first-time welcome; there was Sue, wiry, brittle-faced and morose, who sat in silence and ate and drank everything that was placed before her, then got up and walked out; there was Ida, fresh from the psychiatric ward at Stafford, who told me about the voices she heard, which shouted day and night that she was evil. Then came Dotty and Pol, two elderly widows who came simply for somewhere warm to sit and talk and be in the company of others after they'd done their shopping.

Of Robbo Danks there was no sign, but gradually the young addicts who used his 'shooting gallery' flat began to drift in, in wary ones and twos. Among them were Mike and Sarah Phillips, a well-spoken couple in their early thirties. 'Our little girl's in care, in Manchester, where we used to live,' Sarah explained. 'We came down here to try and make a fresh start so that we can have her back, but it's a real struggle.'

She didn't mention the heroin addiction that was ruining all their lives, and sensing the time wasn't right I didn't press for details. From Ann I learned that the northern couple were unpopular with the other addicts because of their 'poshness', and the word was out that they wouldn't be staying in Chadsmoor for long.

One Wednesday morning Mike came into the hall alone, looking glassy-eyed and with the damp paleness of complexion that I had begun to recognise as signs of the addict 'clucking' for a fix. 'Can I help you, Vicar?' he asked, coming up behind me as I walked towards the kitchen.

Startled, I gave him the next job on hand: placing the cloths on the small tables people had started pushing together for greater ease of conversation. 'When you've done that, you could put the flowers in the middle,' I suggested, trying not to give way to my instinctive unease at finding myself alone with him.

His concentration intense, Mike placed each vase of bright silk flowers carefully in the very centre of each freshly covered table. He stood back, surveying his handiwork, before suddenly turning on his heel and leaving the church hall as suddenly as he had come.

'Is Mike here?' A few minutes later Sarah came in, looking anxious. 'He'd gone when I woke up.' Her hands shaking, she stared blearily at me while I described how her partner had already been in and given me a hand with the tables. To my surprise and consternation, her ashen face crumpled and she began to cry, the slow tears washing down her slim intelligent face.

'I can't believe he went out of his way to do this on his way to score,' she said raggedly, indicating the tables again. 'It's like something he used to do when I first met him – before . . .' Before his life and hers were tainted by the insatiable need for the next fix, I thought, as I tried to persuade her to stay for a hot drink and a chat.

'No, I'd better go and find him,' she said. Before she

hurried out, intent on her own desperate mission for that day's supply, she turned and looked from me to the tables, to the rows of waiting cups and saucers. Almost inaudibly she said, 'Thank you.'

* * *

That day we had a bumper attendance of twenty people. Most of our helpers had brought food to share, and the donation from the Methodist church was being eked out for weekly necessities such as tea, milk and sugar. But as I handed out cheese sandwiches and Maureen's now famous savoury scones, I reflected that if the numbers kept on increasing we were very soon going to be out of pocket. Talk about feeding the five thousand!

'Listen, everyone!' I called, turning off the worship music so that my voice could be heard. 'Before we eat today, and every time from now on, we're going to ask God to bless this food and bless us. Would you all stand, please?'

The tingling I felt told me that this was what the Lord wanted. Yet as they looked up at me, some sullen, some muttering, I reminded myself this wasn't a church congregation, trained over many decades to follow the vicar's liturgical instructions. They could get up and walk out if they wished. That was exactly what one girl did. Tattooed on her face and hands, she pushed the table back and marched out, letting the door slam behind her. 'I'm f . . . ing off!' she yelled down the echoing corridor.

'Let's form a circle and hold hands,' Claudia encouraged me from one side, while Ann, in the middle of a crowd of addicts, held out both arms wide. I took the hand of Ted, Maureen's husband, and was surprised to notice how strong and steady it felt. He, perhaps most of all, was a living reminder that our Wednesday drop-in was for everyone.

The rough circle swayed as I began to say the prayer. 'Ring a ring o' roses!' someone on the far side put in, but the giggle it raised faded away just as quickly.

'Thank you, Father God, for this food and for our Wednesday drop-in,' I said simply and clearly. 'We pray that you will bless us and help us to grow. Amen.'

As the hands were released and the commotion of conversation and the clatter of plates began again, I went to turn the music back on.

'That was nice,' said a rather gruff voice from the corner table. Surprised, I looked up and saw the hitherto silent girl, Sue. She was sitting beside the two old ladies, Dotty and Pol, who also nodded in agreement. 'Yes,' Dotty said. 'We always used to say grace at school, but you don't hear of it nowadays.'

The simple act of giving thanks for the food had somehow opened a door, I realised, as I collected my own rations and joined Sue and her companions. To the right of me I could hear Peter talking to a young man called Darren, telling him that Jesus alone could release him from his addiction to heroin.

'Will you and Ann come with me into the church, Carol?' Peter asked me a few minutes later. 'I want to take Darren in and pray with him in the quiet.'

For the first time ever I didn't seem to notice the extreme cold of St Chad's as Peter, Ann, Darren and I went in to pray, our exit watched by many pairs of eyes, some longing, some curious, some downright suspicious.

'I've known Darren for years, haven't I, Daz?' Peter said, as the young man silently nodded. 'And he knows about Jesus because I've told him before, but what he really needs is to ask Jesus into his heart. He says he wants to, but the smack won't let him.'

We gathered round Darren, laying hands on him and praying for the power of the Holy Spirit to come upon him and give him the strength he needed. Darren was silent, shaking, his hands clammy as John's had been that first afternoon at the vicarage. 'I do want to,' he said through chattering teeth, 'but it's when I get out there – with all the others . . .'

'I'll take you home with me then,' Peter offered. 'Keep you away from them until you're stronger. It's the only way.'

'We'll have to pray hard, because poor Peter's been ripped off so many times,' Ann later told me as we packed the cardboard boxes at the end of the session. 'He was telling me last week he's had addicts staying, trying to do cold turkey before, and they've run off with his stereo – even pinched his vacuum cleaner!'

'Sounds like a blessing in disguise to me, to have somebody pinch your vacuum cleaner!' I joked. 'But I do know what you mean. We'll definitely surround Peter with our prayers over the next few weeks. In fact now the drop-in's actually up and running, I've got a feeling we're all going to need extra protection!'

It had been a good day, starting with Mike and Sarah's moving visit and ending with the prayers for Darren in the church. But the feeling of unease, as if all were not really well, stayed with me like a cloud of warning as I made my way out.

Mark was out and our dog Becky was waiting for her walk, so, ignoring the flashing light on the vicarage answerphone, I put the dog on her lead and set off on our now familiar circular route, down the side of The Nest public house and across the piece of waste ground that backed onto John Street.

When I got back some twenty minutes later, I found a familiar car parked outside St Chad's. Audrey Freeman, a widow in her seventies, who was in charge of the church's two main annual social events, was just getting out of the gleaming vehicle. She didn't smile, and I was uncomfortably aware that hers was one of the stoniest of the stoney faces I'd seen from the pulpit when I'd first begun to broach the subject of an outreach to the needy community.

'I'm glad I caught you, Vicar. I was just on my way in to water my flower pedestals,' she said, holding out the enormous church key in her black gloved hand. 'I also wanted to leave you this!'

From her cavernous shopping bag she took a rolled-up tube, half the size of the church noticeboard. As she unrolled it I realised I was looking at some amateurishly drawn letters on the back of discarded woodchip wallpaper. 'What is it, Audrey?' I asked, trying not to show how my heart was instinctively beginning to fall.

The older woman raised her chin and looked me straight in the eye, somehow managing to convey in that single glance all her disdain about the church of today – so shoddy and inferior to the church of St Chad's as she and all her long departed family remembered it. 'Why, it's the poster for the Maytime fayre, of course!' she stated, as if it were perfectly obvious. 'The social committee asks me to design one every year. And I can tell you that everyone in church will expect to see it on that noticeboard – by this coming Sunday!'

13

The Human Dynamo!

'For God did not give us a spirit of cowardice.'
(2 Timothy 1:7)

'Ah, here she is now!' As I burst, seething, through the
front door with the dog lead trailing and Audrey's poster
held like a truncheon in my hand, I heard Mark's voice in
my study. Still wearing his coat, he held out the telephone.
'It was ringing when I came in,' he explained, as he took
charge of the excited dog. 'And apparently the lady left you
a message earlier on.' Dropping the wallpaper roll onto my
desk, I took the receiver.

'You won't remember me, Reverend,' the caller began.
'My name's Tracy Johnson and I came to a funeral at your
church last year – actually, it was my uncle's funeral. I've
recently started going to my local place of worship, but,
well, I've run into a few problems and I need somebody
to talk to . . .'

The very last thing I needed after my confrontation with
Audrey Freeman was somebody from another parish with
problems. So I suggested, as tactfully as I could, that Tracy
speak to her own vicar.

There was a pregnant pause, followed by a sigh. 'He's one
of the problems, I'm afraid. Look, I don't want to push you
into a corner or suggest you do anything unprofessional,
but I've been praying about finding another church, and
yours is the one that keeps coming back to me!'

'So she's coming round tomorrow night,' Mark noted, as I put the phone down and made a quick entry in my diary. Curiously, he picked up Audrey's homemade advert for the forthcoming fayre. 'What's this? You nearly poked my eye out with it when you came in!'

'You may well ask!' I said grimly. 'OK, it's only a bit of tatty wallpaper with some words in felt-tip pen, but it's going to obliterate half of our Wednesday drop-in notice!'

'I suppose we couldn't expect that sign to stay up for ever,' Mark reasoned, as he led the way to the kitchen and a welcome cup of tea. 'Don't worry, darling. I know you're concerned that we let people know the drop-in's an on-going thing, but we'll find other ways, you'll see!'

The next evening I waited with mixed feelings for the unknown Tracy Johnson to arrive. It had been a long day, starting with a clergy team meeting and progressing, through swift gear changes of emotion, to a crematorium funeral, followed by always necessary hospital visiting. In a kind of daze I opened the door to a diminutive figure in her late thirties, with flowing blonde curls and a dramatic artificial black fur coat. 'Hi,' she beamed, 'I'm Tracy! Thanks for agreeing to see me like this.' My spirits lifting, I felt swiftly ashamed of my previous grumpiness and took Tracy through to meet Mark.

'I've no idea why God led me here to Chadsmoor,' she began once the two of us were alone for our confidential talk, 'but if I tell you my story, maybe we'll find out.'

Tracy's story was a simple one of thwarted discipleship. A nominal Christian since childhood, she had felt increasingly drawn to explore and deepen her faith in recent years, particularly after a failed marriage. 'During that bad time, I just knew that Jesus was with me, holding me up,' she said, wiping away tears. 'I began to read my Bible, and I heard him calling to me, telling me to love people the way he loved us. So to cut a long story short, I started to go to

St Leonard's, and Father Alan encouraged me to attend confirmation classes. The church really needed new blood – new ideas, like mine – he said. The trouble was, though, Reverend Carol, when I actually started to try and do something, all hell broke loose!'

Our eyes met in a smile at the vivid description. 'What, er, did you try to do, Tracy? And it's just Carol.'

Tracy sighed, pushing her hair back over her shoulder as she remembered. 'Well, the church is dead, right? Just a few pensioners who hardly acknowledge you when you go in, and the vicar seems scared to death of them. But outside there's a group of teenagers with nothing to do and nowhere to go. So they hang around and cause trouble, throw a few stones, play about in the churchyard . . .

'I decided to try and start a club for them. There's quite a nice meeting room at the back of the church, and through my work as a consultant I've got loads of contacts, especially for fundraising. Businesses were only too willing to donate sports equipment, good raffle prizes and, most of all, show an interest in this work.'

'Sounds great,' I said. 'And good publicity for St Leonard's too.'

'That's what I thought,' Tracy agreed. 'I've found there are lots of people who, although they don't go to the church, still see it as theirs and were really encouraged to think Father Alan and his flock were trying to do something for the up-and-coming generation.' She broke off and looked down. 'It's particularly close to my heart, Carol, because I've got a nephew, my sister's boy, who has started taking drugs.'

'Oh?' Not for the first time since Tracy Johnson had come through the door I felt my mouth go dry with the undeniable knowledge of the Holy Spirit's presence with us. 'So, what happened about the club?'

Tracy's frustration was obvious as she looked at me

again. 'In a word – nothing!' she said. 'The suggestion was brought up at the PCC and I was invited to outline my plan, or what I was sure was part of God's plan, to invite the kids into the church and show them we cared about them and, more important, Jesus cared about them. But at the meeting it was made clear to me that there would be no support for such a scheme – the congregation felt it was too worldly and too risky. Father Alan said he was sorry, but what I really felt coming off him, in clouds, was overwhelming relief!'

The picture she painted was so recognisable that I swallowed, torn between instinctive sympathy for a fellow priest and angry frustration at the part we have all, clergy and laity, unwittingly played in diluting the gospel for our own ends, and thoughtlessly disabling Christ's body, the church.

'And what about the kids?' I asked. 'Are they still hanging around?'

'Oh yes!' Tracy replied. 'In fact that's what started me praying that God would lead me somewhere else. I was told in no uncertain terms the other Sunday night that I was encouraging yobs and layabouts – the church treasurer's words, not mine; that if I hadn't spent time talking to them and letting them think there might be a club in the offing, they would've moved on somewhere else by now. The best thing I could do, in his opinion – and he'd been at St Leonard's fifty years – was to take my new-fangled marketing skills and go fundraising elsewhere!'

'We shouldn't really be surprised,' I told Mark later that evening after Tracy had gone, promising to pay a visit to our Wednesday drop-in the following week. 'We prayed again this morning that God would bless us and help us to grow. Maybe he's going to use Tracy to answer that prayer.'

'Let's just take it slowly, see how she's accepted, and even whether the project's something she feels led to,'

Mark advised with his usual wise caution. 'You're dealing with yet another strong personality here, and we've already seen that Chadsmoor folk can be insular, especially when they have deep personal problems.'

The next Wednesday drop-in was dominated, as I knew it would be, by people wanting to know what had happened to our noticeboard.

'Our regulars will think they haven't got to come any more,' Ann said unhappily. 'They're so used to being chucked out of shops and so on, they need something that makes it obvious they're welcome – this week and every week!'

'Yes!' To my surprise it was Kenny who spoke up, one of the Baker brothers who were notoriously in and out of prison for drugs-related crime. 'What we could really do with is one of them boards they stand up outside shops. Leave it to me and our kid, Vicar – we'll find one for yer in Cannock!'

'Not before it's lost you won't, Kenny – you're in enough trouble!' Peter grinned. Thoughtfully, he drained his coffee cup and got to his feet. 'I do have a mate who might be able to help us, Carol,' he said. 'I'll pop and see him now on my way home. I'm just going back to see how Darren is.'

As he left, Ann, Deanna, Sheila and I instinctively drew together to say a quick prayer before the cross as we remembered Darren, still struggling at Peter's flat with the demands of his addiction.

When Tracy Johnson dropped in, bringing with her her elderly mother, most of the tables were full and we were struggling, as usual, to keep everyone fed and happy.

'Need any help in the kitchen?' she asked Maureen and Ann after I'd introduced her to them. 'I'll serve, or wash up – whatever you like!'

'That's the kind of help we need, Carol!' Claudia smiled,

coming over a few moments later. 'Who is that lady? We haven't seen her before, have we?'

I shook my head as I rolled up my sleeves ready to start clearing the tables. 'Tracy's been looking for a new church, Claudia,' I replied. Hearing a burst of laughter from the kitchen I added, 'And I've got a feeling she's just found it!'

14
Chips With Everything

'I have learned to be content with whatever I have.'
(Philippians 4:11)

'Chip butties at Chadsmoor!' said the headline in the diocesan monthly newspaper, *Spotlight*. Under a photo of an ill-assorted group of people around a table, the report I had sent in described the venture that now regularly fed and befriended up to thirty people a week, many of them heroin addicts.

The chip butties were a brainwave of Tracy's, after we realised at one of our regular helpers' meetings that serving toast and soup was no longer practical. We were, after all, only a hundred yards from the nearest chippy, and our growing party of volunteers were only too happy to provide loads of sliced bread and margarine.

The chip butties were a great success and we soon had people queuing to collect them, those able to pay dropping a coin into the collecting tin on the counter. Before we ate, I always joined everyone in a thanksgiving prayer, and I was both surprised and touched by the way our regulars, Sue in particular, insisted on it.

'I don't think we'd have got that sandwich board from Christian Peter's mate if we hadn't been saying our prayers,' she confided in me, a little awkwardly, the week Peter triumphantly struggled in with a heavy self-standing advertising board. 'When it says "All welcome", it means "Welcome to our church"!'

'I'm so glad you feel like that about the drop-in, Sue,' I said, giving her a quick hug. Although she smiled faintly, it was like embracing an ironing board, and I wondered not for the first time what her particular story was.

In the village, I heard talk about Specs, who had gone to Plymouth and was living rough on the streets there. 'I hate to think of that, Vicar Carol,' his mother Brenda told me at the Spar checkout one day. 'He rings me up when he can and we both cry, but he is a lost cause, and my husband says he never wants to see him again, not unless he gives up the heroin!'

She broke off and looked around warily at the seemingly ordinary shoppers. 'To tell you the truth, he's scared to come back to Chadsmoor. It's not only the police who are after him round here!'

I already knew from overheard conversations at the drop-in, where people were beginning to realise they could speak openly, that Specs was public enemy number one with the other heroin users.

'He's done the dirty on everybody,' Martin Baker said. 'Nobody speaks to any of us in Chadsmoor now, and it's mostly Specs's fault!'

'He gives all the addicts a bad name, see, Carol,' Ann explained. 'Before he ran off to Plymouth, he'd started visiting an old man in Clive Street, going with him by taxi to fetch his pension every week, then systematically robbing him. Old Wally was terrified of him. Luckily his son found out and put a stop to it!'

'Ar, Vicar, there's some things we don't stand,' Stuart, another of the Baker boys, said. He glanced sideways to where the couple from Manchester, Mike and Sarah, had just come through the door. 'We've heard these two have started nicking kids' bikes from the playground, and flogging them for gear!'

I remembered that most weeks there were news paragraphs in the *Cannock Telegraph* about petty crime, and the stealing of bicycles was regularly reported.

'Most of us have got kids, though we ain't allowed to see 'em,' Martin said as he bit hungrily into his chip sandwich. 'We've all done things – nicked and so on to get our fix – but they've gone too far!'

The following Tuesday Mark and I were woken in the middle of the night by the sound of police sirens and raucous shouting from the car park. 'I can't see any people,' Mark said, going to the window, 'but there's an awful lot of flashing lights out there!'

Next day, the Wednesday drop-in was in full swing when our community policeman Keith Sampson suddenly came in with a woman colleague. 'Just wondered how things were going, Reverend,' he said over the intrusive voice of his radio system. 'Any problems?'

'No. None at all!' The only problem I could see was unfolding before my eyes. At the entry of the two uniformed police, one after another of our regular clients were disappearing through the doors! Noticing the passing scowls and muttered voices along the corridor, I felt my heart sink. Later, Ann said ominously, 'We just can't have coppers popping in each time they're on the lookout for somebody, Carol! I know this Keith chap's only trying to do his job, but look what's happened!'

'It's all to do with Mike and Sarah, I expect,' Peter put in, looking up from where he sat with a very pale and subdued Darren. 'I heard a gang from Robbo's went round and smashed their front windows in during the early hours of this morning. Mike was dragged out of bed and beaten up. He's in Stafford hospital. Apparently, word went round that he'd nicked some kid's new mountain bike and so a posse went after him!'

'Oh no!' I stared at him, trying to imagine the horrific

scene. 'What about Sarah? Was she beaten up too?'

Peter shook his head. 'She's lucky she wasn't because they say she tried to protect Mike, and she called the cops. Anyway, I don't suppose we'll be seeing them on Chadsmoor any more!'

'We shouldn't just abandon them though,' Claudia put in as she finished wiping the tables. 'If you'd like me to drive you over to Stafford, I could do that, Carol. I'm sure Maureen and the others will manage while we're away.' Surprised and pleased by the spontaneous offer, I quickly accepted.

'I suppose this is what Jesus meant when he said we should love the sinner, not the sin,' I reflected a few minutes later, as Claudia's stately old car took us across Cannock Chase, beautiful in its pale springtime colours. 'I've read all I can get hold of about hard drugs, the culture and the resulting devastation in people's lives, but I've still got no idea why heroin is so attractive to people – especially seemingly intelligent and fairly well-educated ones like Mike and Sarah seem to be.'

Glancing at me over the steering wheel, Claudia sighed and shook her head. 'I don't understand it either,' she said. 'In fact, one of the reasons I wanted to help on Wednesdays is that a neighbour of ours has a young son whom Sid and I have seen grow up, and we learned last year he's spending £30 a day on heroin. It's so sad, because he seems to have everything to live for. I've told Simon about the drop-in, but so far he hasn't shown up!'

'There's a Simon in our basket of stars,' I reflected, as she turned onto the busier road leading to the hospital. 'It might well be him, but in any case, tell him he'll be remembered in our prayers.'

At the hospital I checked at the desk and found Mike was in the general medical ward. Sitting fully dressed, his head bandaged and his face grey, he was scarcely recognisable. At his bedside sat his young wife picking at her nails, her head bowed.

They both stared, open-mouthed, when I walked up with Claudia beside me. It was obvious Mike wasn't expecting any visitors, let alone someone from the Wednesday drop-in, where their name was worse than mud!

'I've been trying to persuade Sarah to go and have a cup of tea before we leave here,' Mike said hoarsely. 'She's been hanging about since they brought me in!'

'Come on, Sarah.' Quietly taking charge, Claudia reached for the girl's arm and led her towards the ward door. 'Let's go and find the canteen while Vicar Carol talks to Mike.'

'Shouldn't think you'd want to talk to me,' Mike mumbled, as I pulled up a plastic chair and sat beside him. Turning his head away, he looked towards the door. His feverish need for the next fix was so apparent that my words just slipped out. 'Mike, I do want to talk to you! I-I want you to try and tell me, if you can, well, why . . . .'

'Why I take heroin?' His thin, good-looking face was inches from mine. He hesitated for only a moment. Then, slowly at first, he began to talk, his voice like that of someone in a dream: 'All I can tell you is it's better than anything you can imagine – better than booze, or sunshine, or even sex! It's like being held by your mother in complete and absolute safety and surrender, in a cotton wool heaven that you think you'll never have to leave! But of course you do have to, because the gear wears off, and then you'll do anything – anything on God's earth – to get hold of some more!

'I read a poem once – dunno who wrote it – but it was all about heroin being like a cruel mistress, an evil curse that doesn't let go of you until you're dead. I know that – we all do – and yet the power of it, and the magic, is so strong. You can't resist, because it's only ever going to be for just one more time!'

As he finished speaking, Mike stood up abruptly and lifted his coat from the back of the chair. 'We've got to go *now*!' he said urgently as Claudia and Sarah reappeared, carrying drinks in plastic containers and packets of sandwiches.

'Back to Manchester,' he answered my unspoken question. Then he held out his shaking hand. 'Tell 'em we know we were out of order with the bike,' he said. 'Oh, and when you're talking to your mate upstairs, say one for us sometime, eh, Vicar?'

15
Making Things Official

'For the letter kills, but the Spirit gives life.'
(2 Corinthians 3:6)

'This is great, Carol!' enthused Andy Brown, Rector of the Cannock team ministry, as he looked around our crowded church hall that Wednesday. 'But what are you doing about funding?'

I told him about our first donation from 'Warm Welcome', and how, over the weeks since, just when we needed it most, help had come in, always as an answer to our prayers. 'A little group from Ann's church, Our Lady of Lourdes, has sent us £50, as well as gifts of food,' I explained. 'And every week there seems to be enough for what we need and more in the collection tin, doesn't there, Deanna?'

Our treasurer nodded. 'Yes, we think very often about the feeding of the five thousand, because there's always something left over,' she said, 'and as you can see, the hall has been totally transformed. That's all been done by unpaid volunteers.'

'All very commendable,' Andy nodded thoughtfully as I introduced him to our hall renovators, Anthea, Mary and Brian, who, as usual, had come in for coffee. 'But you could get funding, you know, Carol – have a new kitchen built, and pay for training for your volunteers. This could be a proper centre for drugs work, and you might even have the church modernised into the bargain. You go for it!'

My heart sank in spite of myself as he made a note in his diary to send me details of who to see at the local Council for Voluntary Service. Andy was a great guy, and he was my immediate boss, with whom I should discuss any major changes at St Chad's. But like many other modern clergy, he seemed always to see the business side, the expansion side. His head was perennially filled with great schemes for what the church of God should be able to accomplish in society as a whole, rather than on what God was actually accomplishing right now.

'I'm quite worried about all this funding business,' I confessed to Mark, as we enjoyed a spicy meal at our favourite Dilshad Indian restaurant in Chadsmoor. 'If we think big, like Andy says, we'll have to fill in endless forms and jump through loads of official hoops.'

'You'll also have to nearly demolish the church hall to bring it up to twenty-first-century standards, and in the meantime what's going to happen to the droppers-in?' Mark queried, as he tore off a piece of delicious naan bread. 'It's great to have these schemes. I'm sure Andy's right, there *is* cash available out there. But how many state of the art, purpose-built centres have we seen standing empty because the people they're meant to serve are too intimidated to use them?'

'Or have just got tired of waiting.' In my mind's eye I could suddenly see the Baker brothers trying the rickety door of St Chad's hall and finding it locked, 'closed for alterations'. Then word would get round that the church, like everyone else, didn't really want to know them. And that went not only for the drug addicts, but the elderly shoppers, single mums and mentally vulnerable who had started calling in week by week.

'I think,' my wise husband said, as he poured me a glass

of wine, 'you should eat your dupiaza and leave the future of the drop-in in the hands of the Lord. We know it's what he wants for St Chad's. We've just got to trust him!'

I wholeheartedly agreed, but I was still relieved, when it came time for my visit to the CVS office, that Tracy Johnson was free to come with me.

'I know there are funds available – maybe even lottery funds, Carol,' she said, as we drove along in her car. 'And drugs are such a big problem, it's probably fairly easy to get hold of cash for a project like ours.'

I smiled, gratified to hear the word 'ours', yet hearing another, unspoken word too: 'But?'

Tracy glanced at me through the strands of her bright blonde hair. 'Like you, I'm a bit uncertain about whether we should be going down this road, and you know from the prayers last night that the others feel much the same way.'

I nodded, remembering how, the night before, I had asked all the helpers to come to the vicarage for us to seek God's will about today's visit, and Ann had reminded us vehemently. 'We started the drop-in out of love, because Jesus told us to treat outcast people as we would treat him! That's hard, but it's simple, and what we're doing should be simple as well!'

Mary, who since her mammoth cleaning stint in the hall had even started to attend Sunday Eucharists again, put her hands on her tiny hips, as if ready to take on the world. 'What we really need, Carol, is someone in authority to tell the police not to come barging in like they did the other week, scaring the living daylights out of everybody,' she stated. 'We also need a clear division of labour. Some of us are good at practical things; others, like Ann and Peter, are good at befriending people and praying with them; and we need a reliable source of food that doesn't depend on the volunteers putting their hands in their pockets every week!

That's the kind of funding we need!'

At the CVS, the co-ordinator, Molly Andrews, listened to the story of the Wednesday drop-in with interest. 'I've seen your sandwich board,' she said, as she handed us cups of coffee. 'And all the parked cars, and people going in and out on foot. You certainly seem to have tapped into a community need there!'

I described the amazing atmosphere in the church hall every Wednesday. 'It's almost as if we've – accidentally – started another church,' I said, 'because people of all imaginable kinds just share, not only food, but time and experiences and, well, faith!'

At my last word, Molly held up her hand. 'Before you go any further,' she said, tapping into the computer on her desk, 'I'd better explain that overtly Christian groups are not eligible for some kinds of funding. You are encouraged to have a written constitution, though, and a statement of intent, which is actually called your mission statement.'

Tracy and I looked at each other and I knew I was echoing her sentiments as I said, 'Well, we *are* a church-based organisation of practising Christian people, so our mission statement would have to be based on what we believe God is calling us and equipping us to do.'

'Of course, in an ideal world, that would be accepted as valid,' our interviewer said, beginning to look ever so slightly flushed. 'But what you have to show is that you have recognised a community need, and are responding to that need in a practical, twenty-first-century way! Any religious terminology you should really save for church, because it won't help your cause, and may positively hinder it.

'There are specifically Christian charities, of course,' she went on a moment later, turning to the filing cabinet. 'Here's a list of them, and you'd need to apply to each one individually.'

'I'll take care of that if you like, Carol,' Tracy offered. She took the printed list and put it in her document bag. 'I've joined St Chad's as a kind of fundraiser,' she explained, 'so I'm always on the lookout for acceptable new ideas.'

'I'm glad you said that about being acceptable, Tracy,' I said as we later got back into her car. 'Whatever happens, I'm not prepared for us to pretend *not* to be trying to do God's work at St Chad's – to call it all by some other name in order to be politically correct!'

'So we'll forget about being officially funded for the time being, and concentrate on the more important things that Mary was talking about last night,' Tracy replied thoughtfully. 'Like how we decide who does what, and where we get regular free food, and who's going to tell the community policemen *not* to drop in on Wednesdays!'

'Time for another prayer, don't you think?' I grinned back. In spite of the practical problems we still had, I felt a deep sense of peace as she turned the car through the familiar main street of Chadsmoor.

We might not be tackling things 'formally', but I knew we were held firmly in God's hands and that nothing could prevent his plans from coming to fruition. I also realised, as a rather naughty plan of my own came into mind, that his sense of humour was, as usual, right on cue!

Just before evening prayer I dialled the rector's number. 'I just wanted you to know I've been for an interview at the CVS today,' I began, 'and at the moment the Wednesday drop-in's not really eligible to apply for outside funding. But thanks for telling me about it, Andy.'

'Pleasure, Carol. As I say, I was most impressed by all your efforts,' he replied. 'With six churches in the team, I can't do much, but if there's ever anything else I can do to help . . .'

He was only being polite, but the little voice in my ear

still prompted me on. 'Er, there might be something actually, Andy. You remember how you were telling us at the last team meeting that you've started playing cricket with the chief constable . . .?'

16

Burnt Apple Pie

'In burnt-offerings . . . you have taken no pleasure.'
(Hebrews 10:6)

Mark had come back from an important meeting in Lichfield with lots of news. 'The bishop's suggesting I spend the next few months helping out in the ministry team in central Wolverhampton,' he explained as we set out for our daily dog walk. 'Then, if everything works out, I'll be ordained as a deacon later in the year and take up a curate's post in some other local church.'

'Sounds good to me,' I replied. Black Country parishes are all within a few miles of each other, so commuting from Chadsmoor should pose no other problem but the growing volume of the M6-bound traffic.

As we waited to cross the Cannock road to the ground behind The Nest, I went on thoughtfully, 'I suppose the good old C of E does have to go through these procedures, but you'd think the fact that you've already been ordained, over twenty years ago, would make a difference!'

Mark grinned down at me as he tightened his grip on Becky's lead and led us across the road. 'Ah, but that ordination was done by a Methodist bishop in an American cathedral – not the same thing at all!' he reminded me. 'Anyway, I'm quite happy with the arrangements the diocese is making, and the spell in Wolverhampton will be a good opportunity to learn a few practicalities. The only thing that bothers me is that I obviously won't be around as much as I have been to help you out at St Chad's.'

Mark had been invaluable – assisting me at communion, acting as server when no one else was available, even preaching when I became dispirited at the lack of response. At baptisms he prepared the font, handed out the orders of service and welcomed people. For funerals, if need be, he would step in as unpaid verger. But more important than any of that, on bleak Sunday mornings he'd sit in his overcoat in the otherwise empty first pew, which he cheerfully and even proudly called 'the vicar's husband's seat'. Above all he silently supported me with his love, his sympathy and his prayers.

At the Wednesday drop-in that week I told the helpers about Mark's new circumstances, and we said a special prayer that God would be with him as he adjusted to travelling the ten miles to Wolverhampton each day.

'It's been good to have Mark with us,' said Ann, as she set out the contents of her Traidcraft stall, which she had begun bringing with her in the back of Peter's car. 'Not only because he's a minister, but – well – it balances things out, with so many women here. There is a man I know from church, Carol – his name's Frank – and he seemed really interested when I was telling him about the drop-in on Sunday. Shall I ask him to come and see you?'

I nodded as I went to put some music on. 'Get him to give me a ring, Ann, and then maybe we can arrange for him to come and see what we do,' I replied.

The noise of footsteps coming along the corridor told me that our first batch of visitors was on the way and I knew it was only a matter of time before all the tables would be full, with a separate group outside the fire door that led to the overgrown church garden. There they would sit, heroin addicts, ordinary shoppers and churchgoers alike, some smoking cigarettes, and chatting about how life had treated them this past week.

At twelve noon, before Maureen and Mary went out to the chippy, we would have the short time of worship that had gradually developed from my first words of thanksgiving for food. It usually took the form of a short Bible reading, followed by a prayer for members of the drop-in who we knew were in prison or detox, and anyone who was sick or who had recently been bereaved. This week Claudia had printed a copy of a special poem she had written, all about the drop-in cross. It ended with the words 'Jesus said, "Feed my sheep"' and Claudia had just finished reading it when I realised Sue was crying, her usually silent body bent over the table and racked with sobs.

'What is it, Sue?' I asked gently, going to sit beside her. 'Do you want to talk about it? Shall we go outside, or to the vicarage?'

Sue shook her head. She didn't seem to want to move, but she needed to open her heart, and she did so, pouring out to myself and Anthea, who happened to be sitting opposite, the misery that had taken over her life. 'I-I had a miscarriage – the week before I started coming here, but it's not that. It's my partner, Barry. He keeps saying he'll stop taking the smack, but he needs more and more now just to feel normal – not to get high at all!'

I nodded, recognising the description I'd heard many times now of how the drug demanded everything of its slaves, so that even everyday life became impossible.

'This morning, when I got up, he'd gone,' Sue went on, as fresh tears washed down her face. 'And he's taken all the food money. We've got nothing in the flat, and we're in arrears with the rent!'

While Sue had been speaking, Anthea got up and quickly left the hall. Some fifteen minutes later, she was back, with two carrier bags full of groceries from the Spar. Without a word she put them at Sue's feet. When I later, privately, tried to thank her, she turned to me with tears in her eyes. 'Brian and I are so-called respectable people, Carol, like others round here, who keep themselves to themselves. But this drop-in centre has really opened my eyes. When I look around, I sometimes think Chadsmoor is like Ethiopia, but at least there, when people suffer and starve, they're not on their own!'

Sue was certainly not on her own any more. Her elderly friends, Dotty and Pol, were plying her with fresh cups of tea, and Ann was sitting beside her, telling her she too had a loved one who was an addict, struggling to keep to his methadone programme and hold down his factory job. 'Sometimes the only way we can help them is to pray, Sue,' she was saying when I went back to collect some cups. 'Jesus wants to help Barry – and to help you!'

'I'm beginning to see that,' Sue said, wiping her eyes as she stared again at the carrier bags that shared Christ's love in such an ordinary yet so precious and tangible a way. Reaching out to grasp as many hands as she could, she finished unsteadily, 'To tell you the truth, I-I've never felt such love in my whole life as I feel at this place!'

The words stayed with me over the next few days, lifting themselves into my sermon on Sunday, warming me through funerals, team meetings and school assemblies.

It was after a school assembly that I bumped into a familiar figure I had been feeling decidedly guilty about: Constable Keith Sampson, our community police officer!

'I've been worried I might've got you into trouble,' I confessed, as we shared cups of tea in the quiet staff room. 'After you and your colleague dropped in on us the other Wednesday, I had a word dropped into the ear of the chief constable!'

The young man grinned. 'Not at all, Reverend,' he said.

'We've just been told to approach you personally before we go to the church hall. To be honest, we're not really interested in the characters who come to you. It's their suppliers we want to get hold of.'

As we stood watching the children playing in the yard where school children had played for a hundred years, he explained that he had been asked to speak to the older pupils about his work. 'The idea is that they'll begin to see the policeman as a friend, as past generations used to, and get rid of this bogeyman idea that's so prevalent among the druggies and the other small-time villains,' he told me.

A bell rang, and I put down my cup and looked at my watch. 'I'm glad I've seen you, anyway, Keith. Every success with your class.'

'Before you go.' The policeman looked almost hesitant before he continued. 'Just a tiny word of warning. I'm pretty sure your druggies get their fix before they come to St Chad's church hall, but do be vigilant. Check the toilets for needles or any other signs, and watch there's no passing of little wraps of paper going on around those tables! If drug dealing goes on there, you're the one who's ultimately responsible!'

'Aaargh!' I screamed silently to myself as I turned out of the school gates and, waving to the groups of children, hurried home. Not for the first time, I wished Mark was there. I needed to talk over the scary, just-realised fact that if things did go horribly wrong, I could find myself in prison!

At the drop-in, the atmosphere seemed strained. I quickly told Peter, Ann and the other helpers what the constable had said, and suggested an immediate policy of quiet vigilance and unobtrusive but regular checking of the rather decrepit loos. I had half-expected Ann to protest, saying that such activity would prove we didn't trust our clients and weren't showing faith in God to take care of us.

But Ann seemed preoccupied, the worried look I had
discerned in her face months ago dropping like a shadow
over her eyes. 'Danny stayed out all night, that's all,' she
mumbled, when I asked her quietly what was wrong. From
her bag, she then took several apple pies, each with a
decidedly burnt outer crust. 'Sorry about these,' she went
on, as we all made polite noises. 'I cooked them at 2 am
then forgot they were in the oven!'

As our regulars began to drift in, in twos and threes, I
noticed that for once Tracy hadn't turned up to help.
Going into the kitchen, I began to set out cups and
saucers. Meanwhile, jolly Doreen, who would always be to
me 'the curtains lady', was spreading margarine on bread.
Out of the corner of my eye I saw, to my amazement,
Steve, 'our' drunk, come in with Ann's pretty daughter,
Lizzie. He was clean and tidy and obviously sober enough
to help set up the corner table, where in recent weeks we
had begun displaying Christian books and magazines,
which people could take away.

'Apple pie today,' I smiled at our customers, suddenly
feeling a bit better. 'Ann's made it specially.'

The first man picked up the paper plate without a word,
taking it with his tea to the nearest table. The second man,
though, was Tonto – lean and mean looking. He never said
please or thank you, but regularly went to the front of the
food queue – and if occasionally one of the drug addicts
put a coin into the collecting tin, you knew it wouldn't
be Tonto.

Now, as I offered him Ann's apple pie, he curled his
unshaven top lip. 'I don't want *that* – it's burnt!' he
snapped. 'Where's the chips?'

I wish I could say I thought about Jesus casting out the
merchants in the Temple, or telling Peter, 'Get behind me,
Satan!' But the truth is, I was just incensed. Some of these
people were so arrogant, expecting us to wait on them,

taking our love and service totally for granted! So I eyeballed Tonto, slammed the pie down in front of him and said the immortal words, 'No apple pie – no chips!'

His slack mouth dropping open, he scowled and swore, picked up the plate and swaggered away. Meanwhile, at my side, two things were happening at once. Ann, convulsed with horrified laughter, was clutching my arm, saying, 'Caz, be careful! He's been inside for grievous bodily harm!' And Tracy Johnson, all blonde hair and bouncing briefcase, was coming through the door, announcing, 'Sorry I'm late! But I've found us a baker. And he's going to feed everybody – for free!'

17

Food for Free

'You give them something to eat.'
(Matthew 14:16)

'His name's Paul Tennant,' Tracy explained, her face still glowing with the excitement of it all. 'He's a committed Christian with a bakery only a couple of miles from here, and it's totally amazing! He just happened to be at this consultancy conference I took part in yesterday. Anyway, to cut a long story short, I told him about the drop-in and he volunteered to help out with food every week!'

'Praise the Lord!' Peter exclaimed, laughing aloud, while the rest of us grinned and hugged each other in celebration of another Holy Spirit miracle.

'But how's it going to work, Tracy?' Maureen asked, as she settled Ted with his drink and newspaper. 'And how can Mr Tennant possibly afford to give stuff away like that?'

Tracy gave a little smile and a shrug. 'Apparently, because it's all perishable – filled bread rolls, cakes and so on – he has to get rid of everything that's not sold at the end of each day. So if I go to the bakery on Tuesday nights, he'll make sure I get several trays to bring here on Wednesday mornings!'

Everyone who came into the church hall that day was told about Paul Tennant's generosity and, more important, how that generosity was a response to his faith and an answer to our prayers.

'You drunk, Vicar?' Stuart Baker grinned at me as I danced around to the music, knowing that our noonday prayers today would be a real appreciation of God's love, shown by this unexpected donation of food. Food to be shared, as Jesus had so often shared with his disciples.

'Don't be silly, Stuart – it's only eleven o'clock in the morning!' I quipped back. As I collapsed into the empty seat beside him, I thought back to the time, only months ago, when to be in the same room as one of the notorious Baker brothers would have seemed unthinkable. Now, I could ask Stuart openly, 'When does your case come up, Stuart?' and know he would tell me openly of his expectations of returning to prison, where his elder brother, Martin, was already on remand.

'When I come out next time, I'm going to come off the smack and get a job and a flat,' he went on, his cloudy eyes dreamy. 'Our mom and dad have had five of us, all on the stuff. I reckon they could do with a break. None of us should be living at home now, but the trouble is, as soon as the housing office hear the name Baker they slam the door in our faces!'

In our prayers that lunchtime we held hands and thanked God our Father for the gifts he had supplied that day, and those promised for the future. We prayed for Martin, Stuart and all the Baker brothers; for Darren, struggling to make a commitment to Jesus; for Danny, that he wouldn't be tempted to abandon his methadone programme. In the same prayers we included the sick and the elderly, the housebound of our community – those who would have been astonished to hear themselves mentioned in such a motley assembly of petitioners.

The following Wednesday morning Tracy arrived early and sat in on the midweek communion service, where she attracted several curious glances.

'It's all right, Elsie, she's one of our drop-in workers,' I heard Maureen whisper to one of the most interested elderly communicants as Tracy came back, smiling, from the altar. 'She's got us a load of cakes and buns from Tennant's bakery!'

Tracy later brought in the two big bakery trays as the half-dozen 'regulars' were about to drink their coffee. 'Would you like one?' she invited. Following the example of Fred, who pretended not to see the goodies, however, they all refused downright to accept anything except their customary morning coffee biscuit.

As I followed the little group out to the hall door to say goodbye, the churchwarden turned with a customary parting shot: 'You might be getting the cakes for nothing, but I dread to think what our next electricity bill's going to be!'

I had to admit that while plugging in all the heaters the minute his back was turned, the same uneasy thought had begun to prod at me. Seeing our treasurer Deanna coming down the path, I asked her quietly, 'How are the finances, Dee? Is there any chance we could start paying something to the church now that we're not going to be shelling out for food?'

'I was going to bring that up at our next meeting, Carol,' she said, as Ann came through the door with a slight, smiling man in a cap. 'I'll work out how much we can afford – probably about a fiver a week all year round – and then make an offer to St Chad's treasurer.'

'What did you say about not being able to get the staff nowadays?' Ann challenged lightheartedly. As her companion stepped forward, holding out his hand, she said, 'This is Frank Miller, who I told you about. I've asked him along to have a look at what we do. Frank, this is Vicar Carol.'

Frank turned his head to one side, his blue eyes twinkling. Then he laughed out loud. 'Well, me being a

Catholic I've never really seen a lady vicar close to before,' he admitted. 'But I see you don't have two heads! Ann was telling me you might need an extra volunteer for this project of yours, Carol, so I've come to see if I might be able to help.'

By the end of that first day, Frank wasn't only helping in the kitchen, he had everything and everyone organised. And the volunteers loved it!

'I don't know how he's done it, Carol,' Claudia said, as she helped me pack up at the end of the session, 'but he's already worked out a rota so that there are only ever two people in the kitchen at one time, and they know exactly what they're doing. Apparently, it's all due to his army training!'

After she had driven off I turned to go home, and almost fell over a hunched figure in the portico. 'Peter!' I exclaimed. 'We wondered where you were today. Is everything all right?'

The young man looked up at me and shook his head, and I saw his eyes were full of tears. 'It's happened again, Caz,' he said unsteadily. 'Just when I think someone has really given their life to the Lord – when I've kept them off the smack and prayed and begged God for help for them – the devil gets his way again!'

'Is it Darren?' I asked, and Peter nodded and sighed. 'He cleared off this morning with my mobile phone,' he said. 'I've been searching Chadsmoor for him all morning. That's why I wasn't here. I knew this was the last place he'd be. I was hoping to stop him ending up in a shooting gallery, but I was too late. He's in Robbo's flat right now. After all he's gone through to get clean! Only last night he was praising the Lord for setting him free!'

'Oh Peter!' He was so distraught and exhausted, I knew there was only one place to take him, and that was to the foot of the cross, represented so starkly against the brick of St Chad's.

'Let's go into church and pray,' I said, taking the heavy key from my pocket. 'We've all been working so hard, getting excited, filling the place with the people we feel God wants us to help, seeing our prayers answered. Maybe it's time now just to ask the Holy Spirit to take control, and help us see exactly where he's leading us.'

18

Thank God It's Wednesday!

'Do not neglect to show hospitality to strangers.'
(Hebrews 13:2)

The result of our prayers was the conviction that we should pray even more, in the church as well as the vicarage where our initial MAD prayers had begun. We asked God for wisdom so that we could not only feed the bodies of our heroin addicts but that we would be able to help free them from their terminal slavery by leading them to Jesus. Jesus was the only one who could save them.

Gradually we gathered a whole library of leaflets and brochures about Christian rehabilitation centres up and down the country, and Peter in particular gained heart from the realisation that there were people out there who could help.

'The trouble is, many of these places insist on a commitment to Christ before they'll take anyone,' Ann said after our prayers one day. 'I've tried to get Danny into Carlton Place, the detox centre that's attached to the hospital, but even there the kids aren't even allowed to smoke a cigarette, and if they're found with a can of lager in their possession they're sent straight home!'

'Detox means exactly that, I suppose,' Claudia said thoughtfully. 'To rid the system of all poisons. But these youngsters have been surrounded by intoxicants of one sort or another all their lives. They come from a culture where it's still normal to smoke cigarettes, and booze is a rite of passage!'

'And we're all addicts to a certain extent, even if only to tea and coffee, or chocolate! With me, I don't mind admitting it's a drop of whisky!' Frank put in ruefully. 'Who knows? If all these drugs had been available when we were young, perhaps we would've been in the same shoes as some of our clients.'

'There but for the grace of God go I.' It was a sobering thought that stayed with me long after I returned to the vicarage. 'If only,' I thought, as I prepared for the clergy team meeting, which it was my turn to host. 'If only Sue, and Tonto, and all the others who came to us Wednesday by Wednesday would accept that the grace of God was there for them too – freely and openly offered in Jesus.'

But as Peter had discovered recently with Darren, the 'hard sell' didn't work. You couldn't force people, especially hard-bitten heroin addicts, to make a life-changing commitment to Christ. For anyone to do that, God's timing had to be right, and the need to be healed and saved had to be experienced in a heart that was both broken and repentant. 'Keep showing them love' were the words that came to me as I set out the chairs ready for my meeting. 'And let them help, and not take everything for granted!'

Simultaneously, the faces of Sue and Tonto came to my mind again, the one reflecting surprise and joy at a love she had never felt before, the other cursing as he pushed his way to the front of a queue and was presented with a burnt pastry for his trouble!

The following week, as the drop-in was about to start, I caught Stuart Baker by the arm. 'Go and put the "welcome" board out, would you, Stu?' I asked. 'Peter's not arrived yet and it's too heavy for me.'

'Apart from which a lady vicar shouldn't be heaving lumps of wood around! Get going, lad!' Frank said with a military nod and a bow to me as he stepped into the kitchen. 'I spoke to Tracy last night, Carol,' he went on a moment later. 'Apparently, we've been given a load of goodies from some club that her husband's involved in. A new tea urn for one thing!'

'That'll be a blessing!' I exclaimed, looking down at the rotting piece of lino that had over the years corroded beneath the dripping tap of the old urn.

As Stuart came back, rubbing his hands, to tell me he'd placed the board outside and a crowd was already on the way, my spirits lifted. 'Thank God it's Wednesday, eh, Stuart?' I said, as I hurried over to open the fire door that led to the overgrown garden. Following me, Stuart began to talk about the garden and how he, his brothers and other members of the group had been discussing how good it would be to cut the long grass and get the place landscaped. 'We could make a seat – there, under the big tree,' he said, warming to his theme. 'Even have a barbecue out here when the weather gets better!'

'That'd be great, Stuart,' I replied. As I looked from him to the garden, I thought of an Edwardian picture one of the parishioners had proudly shown me when I first came to St Chad's. 'Do you know, nearly a hundred years ago there used to be garden parties out there, with ladies in long white dresses and hats, and very formal looking men? St Chad's was quite the place to be then!'

Stuart Baker looked at me, his eyes still clouded with the heroin he had used that morning and would have to use again before lunchtime if he weren't to start 'clucking'. 'It still is, Vicar!' he replied, as he abandoned his dreams and went into the still overgrown garden to have a fag. 'As you say, thank God it's Wednesday!'

*   *   *

The manager of the local housing department gave another deep sigh as I repeated my request. 'Yes, that's right. Sue Phillips. She's trying to pay off her arrears, but she's run into a particularly difficult time.'

At my side by the vicarage phone, Sue bit her lip. She still held the eviction notice she had brought to the church hall that morning, and I could tell just by looking at her that Barry's problems with the heroin had got worse.

'The only thing I can suggest is that she comes to see me,' Barbara Allport went on in a deeply patient tone. 'As I've told you before, Vicar Carol, we do all we can to help these people, but if they can't or won't help themselves . . .'

'Go to the housing office and see what you can arrange about repaying the arrears, Sue,' I advised as I put down the phone. 'It might not look like it, but the council doesn't want to evict you and Barry. But one of the things Barbara said was they don't know who else is living there with you, and that makes things really difficult!'

'There-there's nobody who's paying any rent, that's for sure,' Sue said, avoiding my eyes. 'Barry just brings mates, most of them smackheads, and they doss where they can.'

As we walked back towards the church hall, she suddenly said, awkwardly, 'Would you say a prayer – just for me, please, Carol? I've felt better, in spite of everything, since we've had the prayers. Like I'm not on my own any more. And the more you pray, the more I feel like that!'

'That's because Jesus is speaking to you, Sue,' I was able to reassure her quietly. 'He wants you to respond to him by asking him into your heart and your life. Come on.'

As I opened the heavy door of St Chad's and led Sue through the echoing silence to the pew directly beneath the cross of Jesus, I sensed the time was right for her to welcome him. And once again St Chad's felt unmistakably full of warmth and light.

Over the next few weeks, news about the Wednesday drop-in seemed to spread, and our net widened to include people from Hednesford and Rugeley. Not all were addicts by any means, and we continued to be blessed by the sight of the 'respectable' sitting side by side, sharing food and conversation, with those on the very margins of society. 'It's like the pictures Jesus gives us about the banquet in the kingdom of God,' I remarked thoughtfully to Deanna. 'Even Becky wants to come!'

Deanna followed the direction of my eyes to where our dog, refusing to be left in the vicarage, trotted between tables, being greeted by everyone and treated to too many biscuits. 'What really gets me is that so far we've never had anything stolen,' she reflected. 'Given the druggies' desperation for money, I've always worried a bit about that because there are the old ladies' handbags lying around, and the Traidcraft money. It's so different to what we read in the paper every week!'

That particular week's *Chase Telegraph* had contained the news that Darren, to whom Peter had committed so much time and prayer, had been sent down for six months on burglary charges. There had also been a front page 'exclusive' describing how the residents of nearby Bridgeton were up in arms about the activities of the one and only hostel that catered for drug addicts.

Stanley's Guest House was a terraced property privately owned by a middle-aged couple whose son had died from a heroin overdose. Their rule, like more legitimate rehab and detox centres, was that no 'gear' should be taken onto the premises. But I knew from talking to our lads that syringes were left in curtain hems and supplies were passed in other ways from one lodger to another. Now the locals were complaining that the seedy-looking 'guests' were growing in number and contaminating the waste ground near a primary school with used needles. They were also responsible, it was alleged, for the rise in burglaries and muggings in the area.

While remembering to pray for the situation in Bridgeton that lunchtime, I also prayed for the people of Chadsmoor, who were beginning to notice and respond – not always positively – to what we were doing at St Chad's. 'I came past church in a taxi last week,' said one rather grand old spinster to whom I'd taken home communion the day before. 'And there were crowds of really rough-looking people going in and out of the hall! What on earth's happening, Vicar? Someone said they're these drug addicts, but I couldn't believe we'd be harbouring that sort – not at St Chad's!'

As patiently as I could, I had explained to Miss Tregorran that the Wednesday drop-in was open to all, and that St Chad's was God's house, not just the property of the declining, increasingly housebound, congregation who remembered it in its former glory.

'The rough-looking people – and some of them *are* heroin users – actually refer to St Chad's as "our" church now,' I'd finished, trying to ignore the way she glowered and shuddered at the mere thought of such a thing. 'I'm proud that they own it, because if Jesus came back today, it's precisely the outcasts – the real lepers of our society – whom he would make a beeline for, and he'd expect his followers to be with them too!'

Miss Tregorran had sniffed as she handed over her offering envelope and said she'd telephone me when she required the sacrament again. As I left her detached house in Chapel Street, I knew uneasily that her disapproval of our Wednesday drop-in would certainly not be kept to herself. Although not an active churchgoer for many years, Dorothy Tregorran was still regarded with a great deal of deference by both Fred and the lady members of the formidable social committee!

Now, as I finished the prayers, I thought again of Jesus and how he had urged us to follow his example to love as he had loved us, opening ourselves as he had opened himself to fear and rejection and ultimate physical destruction. He willingly embraced all that was deadly, evil and abhorrent for the sake of our salvation.

It was at that very moment that a small crowd parted at the church hall door, and a tall, vaguely familiar figure came, bowed with need and anxiety, right into the midst of us. 'Where's Christian Peter, Vicar?' gasped Robbo Danks desperately, one skeletal hand pressed weakly against his sunken chest. 'I need some help!'

19

The Wedding Blessing

'Jesus . . . had also been invited to the wedding.'
(John 2:2)

'They've kept him in hospital,' Peter told me later that day on the phone. 'His lung had collapsed, so he's on a ventilator.'

'Is he going to be all right?' I asked, still seeing the bowed and frightened figure that Robbo had shrunk into; hearing him plead, as he caught Peter beseechingly by the sleeve, to be taken for medical care, because he was dying.

'Well, put it like this,' Peter replied, 'he's not going to be doing any shooting gallery deals for a while!' He described how, on their journey to Stafford, Robbo had gasped out his fear and hatred for the drug that ruled his life.

'He's used up all the veins in his arms – most of them have collapsed – so he injects into his groin now several times a day,' he sighed. 'I don't know how that's going to fit into hospital routine, do you?'

When Mark came home from a busy day in Wolverhampton, I told him that the Lord had at last answered our prayer for Robbo Danks to be removed from the local drug scene.

'The negative side is there are always another two sad dealers to take his place,' Mark replied. 'As we've found out, most of the users are like Robbo; they cut and share with one another, so technically speaking they're all

107

dealers. But it's quite a breakthrough, him coming to the drop-in when he was in trouble; and he asked for Peter, even though Robbo's threatened and maligned him for months, because he knew Peter is a follower of Jesus and would help him!'

In our prayers that night we thanked God for bringing Robbo to us, and asked God to show us the way forward. We had scarcely finished when a ring came at the doorbell and Ann stumbled in, covering her face with her hands. 'I'm sorry to bother you, Caz,' she sobbed, 'but I didn't know where else to go! I'm so ashamed I feel sick! But-but I had to give it to him – he was threatening me with a knife!'

'Danny?' I queried, and as she nodded I led her into the quiet living room, where Mark was still sitting. 'Come in and tell us all about it.'

'Oh Carol!' Ann looked from one to the other of us, as if trying to get her bearings. 'It's been terrible! I suspected Danny wasn't doing as he should with the methadone, but I didn't realise he'd started going to Robbo's again, doing deals with it!'

'With methadone?' I frowned. 'But surely that's just the medicine to wean them off heroin?'

Ann raised her eyebrows and gave a bitter laugh. 'That's what I thought until I found out it's almost as addictive as heroin and there's a black market demand for it!'

'So Danny's been selling his methadone?' Mark asked, as he brought Ann a cup of coffee.

She sighed wearily and shook her head. 'No, worse than that, he's been swapping it for the real stuff, so we're right back where we started. Except that tonight Robbo's flat's not open and Danny's robbed me, at knifepoint, of all the money I had, to get him a fix in Wolverhampton!'

As the full horror of the situation settled over us all, we drew together on the sofa and began instinctively to pray

again for Ann and all her family, but most of all for
Danny, that God would somehow intervene in what
seemed to be an impossible situation.

The following week I got to the church hall later than
usual, and found to my surprise that Tracy and a group of
helpers were busy decorating the place with balloons and
streamers.

'What's all this?' I asked. Bright music was already
drifting from the player, making my feet tap, and the
garden door was wide open, letting in shafts of golden
sunshine. 'Are we celebrating something?'

Maureen pulled a mock stern face as she placed a large
iced cake on a small table in the corner. 'Don't tell me
you've forgotten,' she said. 'It's Harry and Gwen's wedding
blessing today!'

I hadn't forgotten I was performing a wedding blessing.
In fact, my friend Noreen from Lichfield had agreed to
come and play some special music for it on St Chad's
ancient organ. The wedding couple, Harry and Gwen, were
fairly new members of our Wednesday fellowship. Middle-
aged, with hard times behind each of them that we could
only guess at, they had met and fallen in love against all
the odds and managed to scrape together the cash for a
simple registry office ceremony the month before.

'How much would it cost to be blessed in church, Vicar
Carol?' Gwen had asked me awkwardly. And when I
replied that it all depended on what kind of ceremony they
wanted, she'd looked around and said, 'We've got no
family, so we'd like all *these* people to be there. And to
have it on a Wednesday. Is that OK?'

'Sure!' I'd replied, joyfully making up the rules as I went
along. 'Everybody can come! And on Wednesdays it's free!'

Now, as I watched the busy, loving bustle going on
around me, I was reminded again of Jesus' visions of a
heavenly banquet; a banquet prepared by friends and

shared by a large warm family, with all shapes, sizes, ages and types of people within it.

By the time Harry and Gwen arrived, collected in style in Frank's car, all was ready for them. They were not allowed in the church hall, and Sue, looking pale but strangely at peace, stood in the doorway of St Chad's handing out copies of *Mission Praise* to all their arriving guests. Standing in my priest's robes at the front, I exchanged a backward glance at Noreen, also suitably clad in cassock and surplice, at the organ.

'All stand, please,' I said into the microphone, as the traditional 'Here comes the bride' began to resound through the old church building.

In their simple wedding clothes, Harry and Gwen both looked beautiful, and the happiness that was felt for them was almost tangible. As the happy pair stood before me, Gwen holding the beautiful spray of garden flowers she had been given in the portico, I motioned for the congregation to sit. Almost instinctively, my mind went back to the last time there had been such a congregation here – at Wayne Bennett's funeral. Certainly there were many of the same faces, but today the gloom had gone, and there was an atmosphere of hope and, against all the odds, joy.

'Before we begin,' I said, as a lump rose in my throat, 'we're going to sing a song some of you may remember from school, "Give me oil in my lamp, keep me burning".'

The praise, and the joy, carried all of us through the short ceremony of blessing to the triumphal wedding march, and we all clapped and danced as we followed Harry and Gwen out of St Chad's to a hall that was dressed like the best wedding reception anyone ever had.

'I-I just can't believe all this!' Gwen confessed through tears as Tracy positioned her and Harry by the buffet table for photos. 'They found out the colour of my dress so that they could match the paper cloths and serviettes. And there's even champagne. Where did *that* come from?' I shook my head, caught up in the wonder and excitement that had infected us all.

'Now before we begin our special wedding blessing lunch,' I called, as the company fell dutifully but comfortably silent, 'it's time for us to join hands and thank God for all he's given us today.' I was very much aware that the following Wednesday I wouldn't be around, because it was time for the Lichfield Diocesan biannual clergy conference at Swanwick in Derbyshire.

The days leading up to the conference were taken up as usual with trying to respond to the demands of my role as team vicar of St Chad's, with, as Fred Wilson liked to sonorously remind me, 'the cure of souls'. I visited the schools, pubs and shops, as well as private houses, always aware of how very fortunate I was to have become known to these people by name, and to have also got to know whole families within this close-knit community. But at the same time I sensed a difference in some people's expressions, and greetings were maybe just a little forced. When a woman in the cake shop made some loud derogatory comment about 'bloody druggies', I knew that the disapproval of church people like Audrey Freeman and Dorothy Tregorran was also being expressed in the wider community.

As I later turned for home, I reminded myself that Jesus had told us that following him would not be easy, and that to turn my back on the 'bloody druggies' was certainly not what he intended when he brought me to St Chad's.

'The answerphone's flashing!' Mark greeted me, as I trailed rather miserably through the front door. 'I haven't had time to check it since I got in.'

Surprised, I discovered the message was from the Bishop of Wolverhampton's secretary, asking me to ring him as soon as possible. 'Now what?' I sighed, as I looked up and dialled the number.

My rather disconsolate mood was instantly lifted a moment later by Bishop Mike's cheerful voice: 'I saw your news item about chip butties in the last *Spotlight*, Carol,' he said. 'Would you mind standing up and saying a few words about your drop-in centre at the conference on Monday afternoon – just how it got started and so on?'

I willingly agreed, and then tried to keep my nerves under control. There would be about 400 clergy at the conference, and I wasn't sure what, exactly, our area bishop had planned, or for how long he wanted me to speak.

But on Monday morning I had to admit it was good to leave Chadsmoor for a little while, knowing that Mark would take care of the vicarage, and that on Wednesday the drop-in, once the doors were opened, would operate perfectly well without me.

* * *

The Swanwick conference centre was alive with men and women 'of the cloth' of all ages, sizes and possible human types, and I thoroughly enjoyed renewing old acquaintances and being introduced to new ones.

Then, after lunch, it was time for the first plenary session, during which Bishop Mike invited several of us to join him on the platform. The idea was obviously to share new initiatives, and St Chad's Wednesday drop-in was one of them.

'It actually started through something called MAD – Mothers Against Drugs,' I began, my nerves miraculously vanishing, 'but it's grown so much we not only have addicts dropping in, we have old ladies, single mums, dogs and one week even two goldfish and a barn owl!' I expanded truthfully. 'It's run on goodwill and good news – and people can just be themselves.'

During the tea break several local clergy came up and mentioned they were about to start similar schemes in their churches. 'We should get together, share ideas and pray about where God is leading us,' one team vicar, Doug, said.

'It's actually very exciting,' Thea, another vicar, put in. 'Your experience at St Chad's proves that if we're prepared to step away from the structures and really take a chance, the Lord's more than ready to lead us!'

Bishop Mike came and stood, smiling, beside me, his tea cup in his hand. 'Whether you realise it or not, Carol,' he grinned, 'what's growing in Chadsmoor now is a brand new church!'

20

A Brand New Church

'See, I am making all things new.'
(Revelation 21:5)

'A brand new church.' I couldn't stop thinking about
those words and all they meant. When we began
Mothers Against Drugs all those months ago, we had
no idea of what God had in store for our rather quaint
and somehow unique little community. Looking at the
heroin addicts who came in increasing numbers for
warmth and companionship and free food Wednesday by
Wednesday, I knew that though we might long to 'cure'
them, it wasn't that simple. We were in the business of
sowing seeds, the seeds of Jesus' love which ultimately
led to a loving, all-forgiving Father. For didn't Jesus
himself say, 'No-one comes to the Father except through
me' (John 14:6)?

Bishop Mike's words stayed with me right through to
the following Sunday, when as usual I preached and
presided at St Chad's. 'And what is a "church",' I asked
rhetorically, 'but a place where our Lord's commandment
to love our neighbour means practical things – support for
the elderly, encouragement for the young, warmth and
friendship, fellowship and food? That's what wc've got on
offer now through the drop-in. I do wish more of you
would come along and experience it for yourselves!'

As the tiny congregation filed out, pausing to shake

hands in the time-honoured way, several made genuine excuses for not coming to the drop-in. 'I always go to my daughter's on a Wednesday,' one lady said, while another pleaded a long-standing engagement with her sister. I began to wonder if I was maybe being paranoid. As Fred blusteringly pointed out, *he* didn't go to the women's fellowship, but it didn't mean he was against it!

But the sad truth was that despite all my efforts since arriving at St Chad's, the only increase had been in the number of congregation funerals. Whether the old guard liked it or not, the Wednesday drop-in was likely to be the only 'church' St Chad's would soon be able to offer!

At the drop-in there was always news, and the next Wednesday I learned from a tearful Ann that she had spent several days and nights in prayer for Danny and finally known the Lord was telling her she must withdraw her financial support from him.

'Since that night he threatened me and went to Wolverhampton, I've been too scared to do anything but hand over whatever he needs for the drug, Carol,' she confessed as we sat together in St Chad's. 'But God has told me I can't go on doing that. It's killing any love I had for my son, and any respect I had for myself.'

'So what are you going to do?' I asked, trying to imagine myself in the same position, and failing miserably.

Ann smiled weakly through her tears. 'I've already done it,' she said. 'I've told Danny he's had the last money for heroin he'll ever have off me; that I don't want to see him until he's made up his mind he's really ready for treatment. And I've had the lock changed on my front door.'

'Look! Remember this?' I pulled a crumpled card from my pocket. Through my own misty eyes I read the words from Jeremiah – the promise that Ann had helped me take to the women's groups in Chadsmoor. 'Your children *will* return from the enemy's land! Oh Lord, we claim that now, for Danny, and for all the others who are in the grip of this evil addiction!'

Later, catching up with Peter, I asked for his particular support for Ann over the next few days and weeks. I learned from him that Robbo was out of hospital and expressing an interest in joining us at the drop-in.

'That might not seem much of a breakthrough to you, Carol,' he said as I raised my eyebrows, 'but it shows he appreciates us rushing him off to the hospital, and that the first time he came was literally that – his very first appearance on church premises! He says he'll come next week and bring his partner, Janie.'

That afternoon I was on my way to a funeral visit when I met Claudia coming out of the Spar. 'I hoped I'd get a chance to talk to you,' she said, as we fell into step. 'I understand you're doing the service on Tuesday for Mr Phipps?'

I nodded and told her it was his family I was going to see, and Claudia replied, 'I don't suppose you'll have paid particular notice to the address, but Mr Phipps' brother, Alec, lives opposite me. It's his son, Simon, I told you about, whom I've asked to come to the drop-in.'

The Phipps' house was a neat and attractive semi. The door was opened by a tall smartly dressed woman in her late forties, who introduced herself as Yvonne, sister-in-law of the deceased.

'Here's Vicar Carol, Alec,' she said, showing me into a comfortable living room where her husband sat flicking through the early edition of the local paper. 'Come to see you about your Dave's service.'

Alec Phipps got to his feet and shook my hand. 'Ar, it's been a big shock, Dave dying so young,' he sighed as he indicated for me to sit down. 'He was only forty-five. Heart, the doctor said it was.'

His wife came back from putting the kettle on to ask if

I'd prefer tea or coffee, and her concerned glance led my own eyes to a framed picture on the mantlepiece of an athletic-looking boy with a mop of fair hair. 'Simon, our lad, was really close to his Uncle Dave. He's had his own problems, as I expect you've heard, and I'm terrified this will really push him over the edge.'

'It could have just the opposite effect,' I heard myself say with more confidence than I felt. 'Now tell me all the good things about your brother's life, Alec, and how best he would want to be remembered.'

Simon Phipps didn't appear at the family home that day, but I couldn't miss that mop of fair curls as he manfully helped carry his uncle's coffin into St Chad's the following Tuesday. And on the Wednesday morning he was one of the lads who sat in the crowded portico, smoking and waiting for the signal from inside that the food was ready.

'How are your mum and dad today?' I asked conversationally, as I sat beside him on the rough bench.

Simon looked at me as if surprised by my interest, and then shrugged. 'OK, I suppose,' he mumbled. 'Talking about moving off Chadsmoor again!'

'Oh?' I queried, and it was as if something broke inside him, and he wanted to tell everything at once.

'They keep saying they'll move – get me away from my mates and the gear; that it's the only way I'll ever be able to stop using!'

I thought of the stories I'd heard about addicts finding the strength to break free in a new environment, away from the temptations of familiar haunts and faces.

'Moving might well help, Simon,' I said, as he got abruptly to his feet. I could tell from his agitated expression that he was due for his next injection. 'But look, think of your Uncle Dave – how proud he would be of you making something of your life. Try and do it for his sake, as well as your own.'

What a lecture! I mentally chided myself as I made my way down the corridor. After that, I wouldn't be surprised if we never saw Simon Phipps again!

*   *   *

The following Monday morning brought a telephone call from Ann. 'I just wanted to tell you, Carol,' she said, sounding brighter than I could remember her. 'Danny came round last night looking terrible. He's been sleeping rough and got mixed up with some real no-hopers in Wolverhampton. You're not going to believe this, but one of the girls he met was bragging she'd sold her baby last year – to buy heroin!'

I opened my mouth to say that at least things hadn't descended that low in Chadsmoor, and quickly closed it because only God knew what lay in store. 'And how is Danny?' I asked. 'Does his coming back mean he's willing to really try to make a new start?'

Ann sighed. 'Oh, Caz, I do hope so. I only know I prayed over him last night, and we both cried and he begged Jesus to help him. The thing is, all the family is supporting him now. I told him there were going to be no more secrets from them. Now all we have to do is help him through the cold turkey stage, then try and find him the right rehab place.'

She went on to say that her next week or so would be fully employed with keeping Danny off the drug, and a silence fell between us as we realised just how hard, physically and mentally, that was bound to be.

'Tell Danny we'll all be praying for him, and for you too,' I told Ann firmly.

What with Robbo Danks promising to put in an appearance with a partner, and prayers for an addict on cold turkey, Wednesday's drop-in promised to be one to remember!

21

Disgruntled Voices

'We played the flute for you, and you did not dance.'
(Matthew 11:17)

'Item two on the agenda,' I announced at St Chad's church council meeting. 'Review of the Wednesday drop-in!'

As I'd expected, Fred Wilson got determinedly to his feet. 'Yes. Well, you may remember, Madam Chairman, that the council gave its support to this venture somewhat reluctantly with the proviso that the drop-in be allowed to run for a trial period of six months!'

Around the small semicircle of faces went a series of nods and mutters that I sensed did not bode well for the future of our Wednesday 'church'.

'There are some very unsavoury characters hanging around, leaving cigarette ends in the portico . . . !'

'Yes, and what about the bingo? One of the pensioners could easily be mugged!'

'There are things "happening" in the kitchen too, Vicar!' This last remark came from an obviously irate Audrey Freeman, who rose to her feet and pointed a dramatic finger in the direction of the church hall kitchen door. 'The social committee wants to know where *that* - that cupboard has come from, and why weren't we informed about it?'

I sighed and shook my head, for once wishing Tracy Johnson weren't quite so enterprising about her drop-in fundraising!

'I'm sorry about the cupboard, Audrey. It was, well, donated to us by a firm that one of our members has contacts with. They didn't need it, and we were finding it harder and harder to carry all our things back to the vicarage after the session every week, so Tracy just got it delivered. I'm afraid none of us thought about consulting the social committee!'

Muttering something additional about the tea urn, given in 1960 in memory of one of the Tregorrans and replaced without a 'by your leave', Audrey sat down and mutinously ruffled her agenda papers.

'The point is, Carol,' deputy warden Derek said, in his quiet, thoughtful way, 'we applaud what you're trying to do in reaching out to the community and providing this facility, don't we, everyone?' He broke off and I saw that, Audrey excepted, they all grudgingly nodded. 'But even so, we're naturally alarmed. St Chad's isn't the same any more!'

'Well, hallelujah!' My heart thudding, I got to my feet. 'If we're alarmed, good!' I heard myself exclaim. 'Because that's what God the Holy Spirit does! He sweeps in, like on the Day of Pentecost, and he turns things upside down. I believe that's what's been happening with the Wednesday drop-in, and I'm not the only one!'

Carried along on the wings of my enthusiasm, I told the church council about the support of the rector and Bishop Mike; about an unexpected donation we'd recently received from the Archdeacon's special fund. And, finally, about the surprising telephone call I'd received that very morning.

'The Citizen's Advice Bureau wants to come along and see me about setting up a stall at the drop-in, because some of the people they aim to serve are actually *here* every Wednesday, and they can reach them!' I said. 'We've also got regular contact with the housing department, the hospitals and what few drug services are available.'

I turned and looked from the scowling, bulldog-like Fred to the mild-faced, worried Derek. 'St Chad's certainly isn't the same any more,' I said, 'if you mean it's no longer a safe, closed-up little club that nobody wants to belong to! But whoever said following Jesus was safe? He certainly never did!'

As I sat down, Fred got to his feet. His expected tirade started as usual with the reminder that no one knew more about St Chad's than he did, as he was baptised there seventy-five years ago, and had spent his entire life in and around the place. It ended with his candid opinion that clergy should do what they were overpaid and luxuriously housed to do: namely to take care of the 'cure of souls' in their parishes and not leave their church buildings open to the mercy of all the thieves and layabouts of the neighbourhood!

'Thank you, Fred,' I gulped, ridiculously torn between the desire to laugh and an equally pressing one to cry. 'Perhaps before we take a formal proposal on this matter, we should pause for a moment of prayer.'

As silence fell over the heated tempers and stilled the quick and hurtful tongues, I felt God's presence very near, reminding me how important it was that we do his will. I completely lost the desire to laugh as I began, unsteadily, to say, 'Our Father in heaven . . .'

When I got in that night Mark was waiting. 'Well?' he asked, holding up a bottle of wine. 'Are we celebrating or not?'

I nodded, as I fell into the nearest chair and relievedly kicked off my shoes. 'Jane Jackman proposed the drop-in be allowed to continue for another year,' I reported, still scarcely able to believe it. 'She said how pleased she was, as treasurer, with all the work the volunteers had done in the hall, saving St Chad's a packet in the long run, and that she was more than delighted with the fact that we were paying for our electricity. Then Olwyn – you know, that quiet lady whose husband's funeral I did last year – said she wanted to second the motion because although she hadn't made it to the drop-in yet, she wanted to know it was there for when she did. Luckily Claudia and Maureen are on the council, so I knew we had their votes.'

I took the wine glass Mark offered. 'So although one or two people – notably Fred and Audrey – are now mega-disgruntled, yes, we *are* celebrating for a whole year, I hope!'

'Good!' My husband grinned as he sat beside me. Then, eyes twinkling, he raised his glass. 'It's a double celebration then, Cazza! The bishop phoned while you were out. I'm to be ordained deacon at the end of next month!'

* * *

So much was happening, it was hard to see where God was leading us. As a deacon, Mark would be expected to serve in a parish doing the work of an assistant curate for a year before being priested. This was how the system worked. The parish where Mark was to serve was in Short Heath, Willenhall, a little nearer to Chadsmoor than the central Wolverhampton team where he had been training. He would be able to travel there every day.

I told the congregation of St Chad's the following Sunday and repeated the news to the members of the next Wednesday drop-in.

'Can we go to the cathedral for the ordination service?' Deanna asked, as Claudia eagerly nodded. 'We could hire a minibus, or a coach, and take some of the drop-in clients to support Mark!'

A buzz of interest went round and I smiled in spite of

myself as I saw how quickly Sue, Dotty and Pol put their names down on the circulating list. At a table by the door, his face turned towards all the activity, sat Robbo Danks with Janie, a tiny woman with a permanently cloudy expression.

'How about you, Robbo?' I heard Claudia ask in her polite voice. 'Would you and Janie like to come to Lichfield Cathedral with us to see Vicar Carol's husband ordained by the bishop?'

Robbo smiled knowingly at me, and I thought how far we had come since our first encounter outside his flat. 'What time?' he asked, and when told it would be early in the morning, 'Nah! Janie and me can't get going that time of the day! Thanks for askin' though, Bab!'

In our prayers that day I thanked God especially for the wonderful way he continued to bring so many unlikely people together. 'We are all your children, made in your image,' I said, as the circle of held hands and slightly swaying bodies spread and filled the bright hall. 'And because each one of us is different, unique, each one tells us something different about you!'

Earlier, Maureen had read the passage from Corinthians about us all being one body, and I realised that for the majority of those present it would be the first time they had heard it. Remembering the impact St Paul's word picture had on me as a struggling new Christian many years before, I prayed it would touch someone's heart.

Tracy then prayed for the congregation of St Chad's, that they would lose their fear and resentment of those coming to the drop-in, and I knew she had taken to heart my mention of Audrey Freeman and the alien cupboard!

'Is there anyone else we should pray for?' I asked, giving her an encouraging wink.

Sue immediately mentioned her partner, Barry – that he be freed from his addiction – and this led to others quietly murmuring names, some of which I remembered from the MAD basket of stars.

'Specs, Danny and Ann, Simon, Darren in prison, Stuart, Martin, and the other members of the Baker family.' The pleas rose over the tables and chairs and the laid-out food on the central buffet bar. It was so quiet, with the music turned right down, the sound of breathing and the smell of cigarettes, unwashed bodies and chemical desperation filling the summer air.

Then it came: the crash of the outer then the inner door, and a man with no legs, strapped into a broken wheelchair, was shouting across the floor, 'Say one for me, eh, Vicar?'

22

The Man with No Legs

'I . . . will draw all people to myself.'
(John 12:32)

'It's Karl Butler!' Sue told me in a shuddering undertone,
before I went to speak to the man. 'He lives in that
boarded-up flat down by the railway!'

Karl had already been pushed to one of the tables
and Anthea was busy collecting him some food and drink.
As I sat down beside him, he looked up, brown eyes cool
and intelligent, assessing me and the surroundings in one
long stare.

'So you're our vicar,' he said, manipulating the wheelchair so that he could rest his skinny forearms on the
table. 'I've heard a lot about you and your church for
smackheads!'

Frank brought me a coffee just as Anthea returned with
Karl's lunch. He took it without a word of thanks and I
couldn't keep the edge out of my voice as I replied, 'Sorry.
I haven't heard anything about you, Karl!'

'Oh well.' He paused and raised his eyebrows before
beginning to devour the food hungrily. 'Don't get out
much nowadays, do I?'

A few months before, I would have thought twice about
asking for personal details, but my experience at the drop-
in had taught me that very often addicts are just waiting
for someone with whom to share their story. They are all

too aware that most people would really rather not know. 'So, what happened?' I asked Karl Butler outright, indicating the dilapidated wheelchair underneath him.

The man took a long drink of tea. 'Suicide attempt that went wrong,' he said matter of factly. 'My kid died at six months. He was born an addict. Then my wife ran off to go on the game. I was so sick of the smack I went up on the Chase in my car and aimed it at a tree! Only trouble was, it didn't work, and I ended up like this. Now I don't know what I'm going to do.'

'Is that why you need me to say a prayer for you?' I asked. Before Karl could reply, the door opened and several of our regular members came in, including Tonto and the Baker boys. They all looked surprised to find Karl there, but they gathered around his table as soon as they had collected their food.

'I'm in a flat that's supposed to be empty, see,' Karl went on. 'I'm not the tenant – nobody seems to know where he's gone – and now the council's threatening to put me out by force. I wondered if you'd, like, phone them for me, ask them to give me a bit more time?'

'It can't be right to evict somebody in a wheelchair!' Maureen said, overhearing. 'And it's not as if the council can even reuse the place. It's in a block that's been derelict for ages!'

Armed with this information, I made my way back to the vicarage and rang the now familiar number of the local housing office. 'Barbara? This is Carol Hathorne from St Chad's,' I began, hopefully. 'I'm ringing on behalf of a Karl Butler . . .'

This time the housing officer didn't even try to hide her feelings. 'You've never got *him* there! Look, Carol, I'm sorry, but there's *no* chance of the council giving Karl Butler any more help! He's not only a heroin addict, he's a known dealer. Everybody knows it, and getting him out of that flat is a big part of a concerted clean-up campaign in this area!'

I went back to the hall to find Karl deep in conversation with Robbo Danks. 'I've just been telling Karl about the drugs unit at the hospital,' he said, holding his side as he coughed. 'There's a new doctor there, a woman, and she's really got time for you, ain't she, Janie?'

As Janie blinked and nodded, I reluctantly told Karl about the negative response I'd had from the housing office. 'So it doesn't look as if you've got any choice, I'm afraid, Karl. Can't you go and stay with one of your mates?'

In answer, Karl tossed back his grizzled head and snarled. 'Mates?' he said. 'What are they? No, thanks all the same, Vicar. I'm stopping right where I am! Let 'em bomb the place if they want me out that bad!'

That night, in my private prayers with Mark, I asked that God would break the proud and stubborn heart that Karl had allowed to grow in his disabled body. 'I know he's done terrible things, Lord,' I prayed. 'He's destroyed lives, probably whole families in and around Chadsmoor, but look what he's done to himself in the process!'

More than anything else, I prayed that Karl would continue to visit the drop-in, and over the next couple of weeks that prayer was answered. Like the many other social misfits and outcasts around our tables, he was fed and chatted to and prayed over, and no one batted an eyelid when they knew who he was.

Karl was sitting in his wheelchair with Becky the vicarage dog beside him the day Peter hurried in brandishing a letter. 'Praise the Lord!' he exclaimed, hugging first me and then Deanna, who stood nearby. 'Just read this letter from Darren! It came this morning.'

Wonderingly, I began to read the neat words on the lined prison notepaper. 'I wanted you and everybody at church to know that I've been clean now for six weeks,' the young man wrote. 'But the best thing of all is I go to see the prison chaplain and he prays with me. I understand now what you meant, Peter, when you tried to get me to give my heart to Jesus. I know now that he did die for me, that he loves me and, most of all, that I'm free!'

'Singing in his chains!' I wiped a tear from my eyes as a great cheer went up among the drop-in helpers.

'I think that deserves an extra cake all round, don't you, Carol?' Frank grinned, poking his head through the kitchen hatch.

'It's wonderful, Peter!' said Ann, who had returned to us that day. She broke off, looking around. 'Just think how far the Lord's brought us since we started those MAD prayers,' she reflected. 'If we only help one person to accept him, and get the strength of the Holy Spirit to lift them off the drugs, it'll all be worthwhile!'

Peter's eyes were shining as he asked me for the keys to St Chad's. 'I'd like to go in on my own and ask God's guidance for the next step,' he confessed quietly. 'I also need to thank him for Darren, and ask him to keep him safe.'

After he'd gone, Ann told me privately about Danny's progress. 'He wanted to come with me today, Carol, but I didn't think he'd be strong enough, so I've left my eldest daughter, Emma, keeping her eye on him.'

She described the hell of Danny's withdrawal from the heroin: the cramps, vomiting, pain and sweats; the emotional whirlwind that had caused her home to be in turmoil for the worst days she could remember since her husband had died.

'I kept remembering what that minister told us – you know, the one who works in the prison,' she said, 'about what he and his wife had been through when they kept guard on people through cold turkey. And I've been wondering. Do you think *he* might be able to suggest a place where Danny could go – a residential rehab centre where he could really get his life together?'

'What a good idea!' I exclaimed, taking a page out of my diary. 'Why don't you write to Jim? Now Danny's clean, he really needs a new start, something to look forward to, even if it means leaving home. Otherwise . . .'

'I know!' Ann followed the direction of my eyes to where Stuart Baker and his newly released brother, Martin, had just come in. How many times over the years of their addiction had they gone through prison-enforced cold turkey and then gone straight back to the drug the minute they got back to their cronies in Chadsmoor? 'I'll write to the Reverend tonight!'

The door opened yet again to admit two very different young people: a woman with fashionably bobbed dark hair and a long skirt, and an earnest-looking man with tight curls and blue eyes.

'Reverend Hathorne?' asked the woman, holding out her hand. 'Citizen's Advice Bureau. We rang and you asked us to call in.'

'That's right. You must be Penny and Adrian.'

As Tracy came to take our orders for coffee, I led the visitors to the one vacant table. 'Sorry about the crush,' I said. 'As you can see, we get pretty busy!'

Adrian looked around, his keen eyes taking in the lounging Bakers, Sue and the old ladies in the corner, Maureen helping Ted cut up his food.

'It's certainly not how I remember church premises,' he said. 'I'd like to get involved and see how we can help these people. Wouldn't you, Pen?'

Penny agreed enthusiastically, and I showed the pair the unused section of the hall where I'd thought it might be possible to set up their mobile CAB desk.

Waving them off in their gleaming grey people carrier a

few minutes later, I was suddenly aware of a gaunt, dark-clad figure at my side.

'They're posh, ain't they, Vicar?' Stuart Baker said with decided disapproval. 'What you let *them* in church for?'

Momentarily, we eyeballed each other. Then I waved my hand expansively to the sandwich board standing squarely outside the hall. 'You see what it says, Stuart?' I pointed out, meaningfully. "*All* welcome!"'

23

Ordination and CS Gas

'Rekindle the gift of God that is within you.'
(2 Timothy 1:6)

Mark's ordination was attended by all the helpers of the drop-in, plus a few of the elderly clients and the team rector, Andy Brown.

'I'm glad you had a spare seat on the minibus, because I wanted to talk to you, Carol,' he said as we squashed into the two front seats with our church robes. 'I'm hearing good reports about the drop-in, and it makes me realise that actually your job description is way off the mark!'

'Why's that, Andy?' I asked, as we turned out of the drive and took the road to Lichfield.

'Well,' the rector leant his head back, his thoughts obviously soaring into the future, 'what's really needed in a place like this is not a team vicar with sole responsibility for the church, because the church, let's face it, is on its last legs – and I know you've done your best to change that! No, now the Wednesday drop-in's up and running, your work should take you about seventy per cent into the community with the addicts and other problems, and thirty per cent in the church. It's a job that someone with a real drugs awareness background would jump at actually!'

'Trying to get rid of me, are you?' I quipped. As he quickly denied it, I realised that what he was saying did actually make a lot of sense. Trying to run St Chad's, with its occasional offices and moribund meetings, sometimes seemed an impossible task on top of the increasing demands of the drop-in.

As we all later filed into Lichfield Cathedral and the moving service began, I tried to concentrate on the beauty and wonder of these moments of giving and receiving the gifts of ministry, and to forget that once Mark officially belonged to Short Heath, Willenhall, doing the unsocial hours of an assistant curate, we would scarcely see each other at all.

The next Wednesday drop-in brought news that Karl Butler had been evicted by the council and police using CS gas.

'Didn't you see it in the paper last night?' Mary asked, as she swept the floor between the tables. 'There was a picture of him in the wheelchair and a big headline saying "Disabled junkie defies police bombs!"'

When he came in, Karl looked almost apologetic. 'I know you can't do nothing – the authorities've shown what they think of me,' he said, cradling his hands around the mug of tea Claudia had given him. 'I slept under the railway bridge last night, but I just thought you'd want to know I'm still alive, like . . .'

I swallowed. 'I do. We all do,' I squeaked, realising it was true.

When Ann came in, followed by Frank and Tracy, I drew them together at another table. 'Look, I know he's a villain,' I said, 'but Jesus had time even for the thief on the cross! So we can't condemn anybody. He shouldn't sleep under the railway bridge again tonight, not in his state!'

Tracy, fired by the challenge, was already taking out her mobile phone. 'I know somebody with some ground floor bedsits in Rawnsley,' she said, 'but they're not furnished . . .'

'We'll soon collect enough stuff for a bedsit,' Ann said.

'I've got a table in my cellar I don't use any more, and I think Frank's got a spare mattress!'

'What about that carpet that's been rolled up by the portico door for months?' Claudia asked. 'Couldn't we take that, Carol?'

I hesitated, still remembering the contentious cupboard. 'I'd have to ask Fred,' I said, 'but yes, all that old carpet's doing is gathering dust!'

At the end of that day, to the total amazement of both Karl Butler and myself, the crippled man was almost ready to be rehoused, his first week's rent paid out of drop-in funds, the majority of needed furniture found.

While Peter prepared to take him to Rawnsley, I rang Fred Wilson to ask if we could have the disused vestry carpet.

'I suppose so,' he said grudgingly, 'but make sure that's all that gets taken. We've lost things that way before!'

While I was telling myself it was impossible for Fred to be any more objectionable, he proved me wrong. 'I've been thinking about your husband's new job! In normal circumstances his new parish would have to find him a curate's house, so as he's living here in *our* vicarage, we'd be within our rights to charge Short Heath parish rent!'

'A-a-a-a-r-g-h!' I screamed as I put the phone down, terrifying the dog. Telling myself I wouldn't mention Fred's suggestion to Mark, I hurried back to the church hall to tell Karl he now had a carpet!

'I'll go over tomorrow and help him sort out his benefits and so on,' Peter said, when he called at the vicarage to let me know Karl was safely moved. 'I've told him I'll collect him for the drop-in every week too, if he still wants to come. I know some people would think we're just letting him, and the others, take us for a load of suckers, but more hardened druggies than Karl have cracked under the love of Jesus!'

Peter went on to tell me about an idea the Lord had given him after his letter from Darren. 'I've got the video series *Jesus of Nazareth*, and I thought we could advertise that I'd be showing it at my place every week from now on. There's one or two people already said they'll come along.'

Over the next few weeks, the activities at the drop-in took another unexpected turn through a telephone call I had from the local hospital. 'Our drugs unit is ready to do anything to help the local addicts, Reverend Hathorne,' the young lady co-ordinator explained. 'We already provide a needle exchange and, of course, methadone programmes. But there's something new that we'd really like to try, and your drop-in centre sounds just the place to do it!'

To my surprise and slight consternation, the innovation was the ancient Chinese art of acupuncture. And that was how, one Wednesday morning in October, a group of supervised Chadsmoor heroin addicts were to be found in a screened-off corner of the hall, all fast asleep with long needles protruding from their ear lobes – a process meant to help break the addictive pattern of their days.

'I can't believe it!' Claudia whispered, as we tiptoed away. 'Those chairs aren't comfortable to sit on, let alone use as beds!'

We had both been encouraged to see her neighbour's son, Simon, taking advantage of the offer of the free session.

'I pray for Simon every day,' Claudia told me, as we went back to the noisy part of the hall. 'I know he's got it in him to make a new start. He just needs the incentive.'

That was true of so many of our clients. Their lives had become so bound up in the demands of the daily fix, sometimes up to ten fixes a day, that they had lost all other reason to live. Although I knew that as Christians we have to be careful with 'alternative' practices such as acupuncture, in this case I felt after much prayer it was right to go ahead.

The weekly paper continued to carry stories of drugs-related crimes and court cases, and many of the names were now known to me. I was still taken by surprise, however, by the visit of our policeman, Keith, early one Monday morning.

'I'm afraid there's a nasty con merchant around, Reverend Hathorne,' he began, as I led him into the vicarage. 'He knocked on the door of an old lady's bungalow up the road last night, and she let him in because he said he was from St Chad's Church and she'd won a prize! He then took off with her pension book with a load of money in it. What makes it worse is she's suffering from terminal cancer!'

The crime victim, Lily Deakin, was being cared for by her neighbour when I called to visit her later that day. 'He said he was from St Chad's, and you were trying to help the sick and needy,' the neighbour said with concern as I went closer to the white-haired old lady. 'Then he told Lily she'd won a microwave!'

'I thought it was funny,' Lily put in quaveringly, 'cos I've never bought any ticket. In fact I haven't been out for ages, have I, Gladys?'

'No, love,' Gladys shook her head. 'The police seem to think it might be one of the druggies,' she told me with a sniff. 'They'll do anything for money, and we seem to be getting more and more in these parts lately!'

Before I could reply, Lily put out her hand to me. 'Anyway, Vicar, this trouble apart, I'm glad you've come because I wanted to see somebody from the church – about me arrangements . . .'

Gladys took this as her signal to leave, and Lily and I spent the next half-hour talking and praying together.

'I'm not afraid to die – not at all, because I'll be with my Charlie again,' Lily said as I sat holding her bird-like hand. 'But I do want things right for the service, and now I know you'll be taking it I feel much easier in my mind.'

'I wish *I* did!' I thought silently as I turned back towards St Chad's. I wondered just who was the young scruffy-looking man who had tricked his way into Lily's bungalow using our name as a lever. Although, like Lily herself, I could see God's hand in bringing us two together, the crime was so despicable, and the betrayal, if it was one of our lads, was really hard to deal with.

Trying not to think about the gossip that must even now be buzzing around the Chadsmoor shops, I let myself back into the vicarage and telephoned Ann. 'Can you pass the word on?' I asked, after telling her Lily's story. 'And just mention that if such things carry on, we're likely to lose the drop-in altogether.'

By the next Wednesday morning, a new word was going around the village. Lily Deakin's robber had been arrested after trying the same trick using the name of St Peter's Church, Hednesford. He *was* a drug user, but he came from far off Rugeley!

'I didn't think it could be a Chadsmoor lad, Carol,' Ann said, as a queue began to form from the portico door right along the church hall corridor. 'They know they've got too much to lose!'

24

A New Start

'So if anyone is in Christ, there is a new creation.'
(2 Corinthians 5:17)

'Can we talk in church?' Sue asked me quietly. 'Only I've got something important to tell you.' The young woman had looked paler than ever in recent weeks, and it had been on the tip of my tongue to ask how things were with her partner, Barry.

'I can't believe it, Vicar Carol,' she went on, as we sat down in the silent coolness of the old brick church, 'but I'm pregnant again, and this time I'm going to do all I can to keep it!'

'That's great news!' I exclaimed, giving her a hug. 'Our first drop-in baby! What does Barry say?'

Sue hung her head. 'That's what I wanted to talk to you about,' she said.' I've prayed and prayed and I think God is telling me to make a new start, away from Barry. I've given him so much over the years. I-I've even been a prostitute to get money for his habit. But all he cares about is heroin. He wasn't bothered when I lost the last baby, and he just shrugged his shoulders when I told him about this one!'

'Oh Sue, I'm sorry,' I said, seeing the pain in her eyes. 'But look, this new start . . .'

'The new start is with God, as well as the baby,' the young woman said shyly. 'Since I let Jesus into my life, I've felt such hope, and I want my baby to have that hope too – not grow up into a victim, the way I have!'

Sue and I prayed together, asking God's blessing and protection on her and her unborn child. Practically speaking, I knew the next step was to approach the housing department on her behalf, and this time Barbara Allport was only too pleased to assist her.

'From what I've seen of her partner, he'll scarcely know she's gone,' she said bluntly, 'but you must tell her to come and register here as homeless. That's the first step.'

'Looks as if we'll be scouting round for furniture again,' I told Mark that afternoon. 'Hopefully, Sue will be re-housed very soon.'

Then I stopped and looked from him to the clock. 'Hey, why are you home so early? And why are you looking so worried?'

In answer, Mark took the dog's lead from the cupboard. 'Time for Becky's walk, I think,' he said seriously. 'We'll talk as we go.'

Outside the church hall, Frank and Tracy's cars were still there and the busy figure of Mary was seen emptying a mop bucket into the drain.

'I thought the drop-in finished at two?' Mark queried.

I grinned. 'It does, but they keep on finding jobs to do,' I replied. 'At the moment, it's all systems go for Christmas – that's only a few weeks away. Good thing I can leave all the arrangements to the helpers, what with all my extra services!'

Mark's worried look deepened as we crossed the road and let Becky run on the waste ground. 'It looks as if I'll be having extra services soon too, darling,' he said. 'The bishop dropped in to our staff meeting this morning. Apparently I've been head-hunted for one of the team vicar's jobs there in Short Heath! Because of all my experience, they don't see the need to wait the usual year for me to be priested. The only thing is . . .'

'They need you to live in the parish of Short Heath, and not in Chadsmoor,' I finished quietly.

Mark nodded and sighed as we fell into step. 'Well, yes, and of course it makes sense. Once I'm licensed as vicar I will have, in Fred's famous words, "the cure of souls" and I'll need to be instantly available. There's a vicarage there, you see, that's been empty now for nearly two years . . .'

'But you can't live there on your own!' My heart sank at just the thought of that. 'Look, I know younger clergy couples sometimes manage to combine two incumbences – and two houses – and just see each other weekends, but I can't believe that's what God wants *us* to do!'

'We need to pray hard about it,' Mark said. 'And like always, we'll do what we really feel the Lord is calling us to do. OK?'

That night we lit our candles and said Evening Prayer in the vicarage, and as we prayed it became clearer and clearer that our combined future ministry lay with Mark at Short Heath.

'I know I was brought to Chadsmoor to help start the Wednesday drop-in,' I said, reaching for a tissue to dry sudden tears. 'But God keeps reminding me of what we saw today after the session was over. The helpers know him and are being led by him in this work. They might think they need me, but they don't really, and that's the great strength of the Holy Spirit!'

'Yes!' Mark pulled me into his arms for a cuddle. 'Remember St Mark's Sunday school. That still carried on and became healthier than ever, even though you left to come to Chadsmoor!'

As we finished our prayers, I felt, in spite of my sadness, the beginnings of a deep sense of peace. This was God's work that we had been privileged to help put into operation. Only he knew the future he had planned for it.

*   *   *

The official announcement that I was leaving St Chad's went out two weeks before Christmas. No one in the congregation seemed surprised, and one or two people said they had been expecting it since Mark's ordination. The question on everybody's lips was, 'What will happen to the Wednesday drop-in?' A question which was obviously first asked at the private pre-announcement meeting I had with Ann, Peter and other trusted helpers.

'It's going to continue, of course!' was my firm reply. 'Andy's assured me of that, and I know he's got ideas he's going to put to Bishop Mike about the job description of my successor. Anyway, I'm not leaving for three months, so we've got plenty of time to plan!'

'Oh Caz, we'll be really sorry to see you go!' Ann said sincerely, as Maureen and Claudia nodded. 'So much has happened since we've been working together! Look at my Danny – doing so well at that place in Sheffield. He's like a different lad, and it's all thanks to the Wednesday drop-in!'

Another pre-announcement meeting had, of course, been the small but official one with my churchwarden and deputy.

'What did I tell you?' Fred looked almost triumphantly at Derek. 'I told him you'd be off within the next year!'

'Yes,' Derek sighed. He didn't look at me as he said, 'So St Chad's is going to be without a vicar again. Well, never mind. We're used to coping in an interregnum, aren't we, Fred?'

Brusque Fred brightened up at the prospect, rubbing his

hands together. 'We are! For some reason the dog collars come and go pretty fast! Some have only stayed twelve months or so!'

While they began to calculate how many clergy had been through the treadmill at St Chad's, I went out to put the kettle on. I calculated my term would be three-and-a-half years by the time I left in March. In many ways it seemed much longer.

By the time the next drop-in came round, people in the village knew I was leaving. Frank, coming in with Ann, stopped me with a mock stern expression as I walked into the kitchen. 'What's this I've been hearing about you, Vicar Caz?' he demanded, eyebrows quizzically raised. And when I told him it was true, 'I know what I'll do, I'll write to the Pope! That'll stop you!'

The business of the day soon took over and I was able to tell people the news about our move in a natural way as I flitted, as usual, from table to table.

'But where will *your* church be?' asked Doreen the curtain lady, as we reassembled after our lunchtime prayers. 'Won't you be a vicar any more?'

I grinned. 'I reckon once a vicar always a vicar,' I said, 'but the way we feel the Lord is leading us is for Mark to remain in full-time paid ministry and me to apply for a licence to officiate, which means I can take services but won't be responsible for any church . . .'

'Or church building, or church council, eh?' Claudia put in thoughtfully. 'I really don't want you to go, Carol, but I can see how much God wants to release you from all that!'

'I've also got another ministry, you know,' I went on, feeling slightly foolish, but unable to ignore the nudgings of the Holy Spirit any longer. 'The ministry of writing about what I see God's actually doing. And once we get to Short Heath, I should be able to find time for that again. Anyway, that's enough about me. What are we going to do about a Christmas service?

*   *   *

The Wednesday drop-in's first ever carol service took place the following week. 'There's never been a carol service like this!' Noreen, our now official drop-in organist, whispered as we bowed to the altar and I went to announce the first song.

I looked around icy St Chad's, and a wave of warmth and interest rose up to meet me. Gathered here for our celebration of carols, prayers and readings were all the members of our Wednesday fellowship.

Noreen struck up 'O little town of Bethlehem' and at my signal everyone stood and sang. The two dogs, Becky and Maureen and Ted's Millie, each contentedly stretched out on separate sides of the aisle.

As I sat down, Ann, looking better than I could ever remember, came forward to do the first reading. Meanwhile, Sue, delighted to be asked to help, stood at the door handing carol sheets to latecomers.

'Shall I start now, Carol?' said a tall, gangling man coming forward carrying a guitar.

I nodded. 'Yes. Thank you, Tony.' Standing up, I spoke into the microphone. 'Tony, who some of you will know from Peter's video meetings, is going to sing his favourite song: "My Jesus, my Saviour".'

As the melodious chords began and Tony sang his heart out, I caught Peter's grin from the front row. I remembered how Tony, a Christian from a Hednesford fellowship, had come to us, bringing along his manic depressive son, Andrew.

Winter sunshine suddenly broke through the stained-glass window, illuminating the cross of Jesus, the focal point of this old and sombre place. But it shone too on the crib scene, assembled, as in other years, in the box of the turned-round wooden altar. It reminded us of the coming joy of our Saviour's birth.

'Right, everyone!' I said, as my heart swelled with too many emotions to disentangle in one day. 'We stand and sing "O Come All Ye Faithful", number 22 on your sheet. And then it's back to the hall for our Christmas party!'

25

Christmas Joy – and Terror

'Do not be afraid . . . I am bringing you good news.'
(Luke 2:10)

Midnight mass was special, the congregation swelled with those who hadn't been to St Chad's since last Christmas Eve. Many of the faces were familiar, from weddings and funerals, and there sat the young couple whose baby daughter I had baptised a few weeks ago as 'Willow Anastasia'. Now there was a name to conjure with.

By communion time the pubs would be closed, and I knew there would be other people shuffling or bursting noisily in, making their unsteady way up to the altar that was a detour for them on this one night of the whole year. As I went up the stone steps into the pulpit, I caught sight of the hunched figure of Andrew, the disturbed son of Tony. Tony was singing for us again, breaking the tradition of St Chad's Midnight Eucharist, which had once been a very solemn, grand affair.

Near him sat others from the Wednesday drop-in. Doreen wearing a red scarf with the words 'I love Jesus' all over, and her sister Mary, for once quiet and still. Sue, her skin glowing in the icy air, was like someone reborn now she had a new home and a new life to look forward to. Others, like Frank and Ann, were at their own churches tonight, but Peter had asked particularly to be here, to lead the prayers.

'I want to thank God for all he's doing in Chadsmoor, Carol,' he said simply. 'I know we won't get any of the addicts – at that time of night most of them will be flat out one way or another, and we've got to accept that. But those people who do come need to hear how great our God really is, and that he's their God too.'

'You took the words out of my mouth!' I replied. Now, as I looked down at the various calm, expectant and apathetic faces, I prayed that God would give me new words. I remembered Jesus' promise that the Holy Spirit would speak through those who were on trial for their faith. Rightly or wrongly, I felt I was on trial right now, needing to justify the work among heroin addicts that St Chad's was doing; needing to explain that I personally would not be around after the first Sunday in March; above all, needing to convict once-a-year worshippers of *their* responsibility towards God's house.

'Whenever people know I'm from St Chad's,' I began, 'they say two things. "Is it still as cold in there?" and "I went once, and nobody spoke to me!" But you're all in St Chad's tonight because you feel the need, the very real, deep need, to worship on this night of all holy nights, when our Lord Jesus came into the world as that baby in the manger!

'Some of you were here last year, and the year before, and maybe you think that's enough to show your gratitude to God and be members of his church. But I'm here to tell you now that unless you do more than turn up once a year for midnight mass, St Chad's won't be around much longer. With the present congregation of twenty, I calculate that this church – your church – will be closed within five years!'

At the end of the service I was approached by Derek, who had been sitting in the warden's pew near the door. 'I'm glad you said what you did, Carol,' he said, surprisingly, and I realised he felt he could speak openly because the overbearing Fred wasn't there. 'People need to realise that the church they remember from childhood isn't still there, set in aspic somewhere, just for special occasions.'

'Jesus came to make every day special, Derek,' I said, my heart lifting. As I watched the people leaving, calling 'happy Christmas!' to each other, I knew that if I had made that one point in my last midnight sermon, it would be more than enough.

*   *   *

After Christmas came the usual lull, with clergy colleagues on holiday and the crematorium and other public buildings closed. We opened the drop-in as usual on Ann's insistence.

'This is the worst time for people with problems,' she pointed out. 'Everybody stuffed and snoozing off the Christmas cheer – a sense of depression and failure everywhere. I know Tennant's won't have buns for us this week, but let's do some jacket potatoes and bring them in wrapped in foil!'

Numbers were down that Wednesday: Dotty and Pol were with their families, Doreen and the church hall workers were busy at home. The addicts drifted through in ones and twos. Seeing Steve, 'our' drunk, on his way down the corridor, I prepared a place at the table, still decorated with Christmas candles. Steve was swaying and crying, as he had been on his first visit.

While Peter made him some black coffee, Ann took me to one side. 'I tried to take him to the doctor's a couple of weeks back, Carol,' she explained, 'but they said he's been banned again, this time for trying to drink the cleaning fluid in the gents' toilet there!'

'Oh no!' As I watched Peter trying to get the other man to drink his coffee, praying over him as he did so, I thought of other attempts that had been made to reach Steve. Through Ann's Lizzie, there had been Alcoholics Anonymous, counselling and many, many prayers. Like the other victims of alcohol and drug abuse that we fed now on a regular basis, Steve needed to know Jesus and the life-changing power of his Holy Spirit. And for that he had to be open and willing and, above all, ready to receive.

*   *   *

That December afternoon, I went home and began to make lists of all the things we had to do before our move to Short Heath. Mark had been called out to the hospital over there, and I was alone in the vicarage apart from the dog.

Suddenly, she started to bark and I realised with a start that outside the windows it had gone very dark. Everywhere seemed eerie and silent, reminding me of the isolation of the house, hidden as it was behind the big church.

'Vicar! Vicar! Open the door!'

'We need some money!'

'No – food! We need food!'

'We missed the drop-in today!'

As the men's voices rose, Becky's hair came up all along her back. I stood in the living room, frozen to the spot. A voice inside told me, clearly and protectively, that on no account must I open the front door.

The bell jangled, the voices came again, more insistently,

edged with angry desperation: 'Open the bloody door, Vicar!'

Then, to my heart-stopping horror, 'It's open!' a man's blurry voice exclaimed. Too late, I realised that the outer door had indeed been left unlocked, and four big heroin addicts, including the menacing Tonto, were filling the porch and hammering with their fists on the corrugated glass panel!

Eventually they left, cursing and 'clucking', screaming at one another in their need for the drug they had been unable to get hold of because of the demands and excesses of the Christmas season. As an afterthought, one of them came back and gave the door a running kick.

By the time Mark came back, I'd found the courage to go out and lock the outer door and was sitting with all the lights on and the curtains drawn. 'Just-just get me away from this place!' I sobbed, shaking from head to foot. 'I'm really, *really* scared!'

26

A Banquet to Share

'Come; for everything is ready now.'
(Luke 14:17)

'Just look at that for a headline!' Claudia beamed when I saw her in church the following Sunday. Ignoring the scowling Fred, she handed me the *Chase Telegraph*. 'Church aid to Druggie Evangelist!' screamed the front page. '"I want to tell people about Jesus," says cured heroin boy, Darren.'

Privately thanking God for this wonderful encouragement, I listened as Claudia described how she had bumped into Peter the day before, and he had told her Darren was out of prison, still 'clean' and still on fire for the Lord.

'It's Peter's church that's sponsoring him,' she said. 'He's going to be given living expenses and hopefully a chance to study, and maybe eventually go into some sort of ministry with young people!'

'That's just wonderful – another answer to one of our very first MAD prayers,' I said. Mark and I would be going to the Baptist church for a special New Year praise service that week, and I guessed rightly that Peter and Darren would feature greatly in it. First, though, I had promised to visit Lily Deakin, and as I set out along the street, I reflected on how close to the old lady I had grown since the robbery that brought her to my attention.

One of the first things she said after her neighbour let

me into the bungalow was, 'I'm glad it wasn't one of your church people that took my pension, Vicar Carol. He was a villain from off, wasn't he?'

I took her paper-thin hand. She was growing more fragile every time I saw her. 'Yes, Rugeley's definitely off,' I said, 'though we're not short of villains of our own, are we?'

Lily shook her snowy head. 'No, and it hadn't used to be like that! We had proper gentry on Chadsmoor – the Tregorrans. I worked in one of their shops, and their father had a pony and trap for rides up on the Chase!'

I remembered the sepia photographs I had talked to Stuart Baker about, with scenes on the vicarage lawn. How different the area around the church was now, particularly on Wednesdays!

Later that day I walked up to the Spar, spending a few minutes, as usual, talking to Brenda Ellis.

'John's still away,' she said in answer to my question. 'Sometimes when he rings he'll say he's in Bristol, then it'll be Southampton. We don't know what to believe. But, oh, Vicar Carol, something else has happened since I last saw you – something brilliant!'

Putting a hand in her overall pocket, she pulled out a photograph. 'This is my grandson, Ben,' she said, almost visibly swelling with pride. 'My daughter gave birth to him on December 15th. Isn't he *gorgeous*?'

I grinned, her joy infectious. 'He is,' I agreed, 'and he's obviously done you a power of good!'

Brenda nodded. She stared down at the photograph. 'Ben's a new lease of life for his granddad and me,' she said. 'Our Lesley wants us to help look after him while she goes back to work and, well, it's like a new start!' She broke off and reached for a tissue. 'God's so good, isn't he?'

Over the next few weeks, our final ones at Chadsmoor,

God proved his goodness time and time again. The drop-in membership grew, with the provision of housing and CAB advice, counselling referrals and support for court and doctors' appointments available as well.

After my post-Christmas scare, I was almost afraid to look some of our clients in the eye, but somehow, without anyone actually making an apology, it was made clear that a group of the lads had been in a bit of a state and stumbled to the vicarage when they found the church hall locked.

'We can't be open all the time!' Ann said. 'Though from what the rector plans, we *could* be, a few years down the line! You just make sure you leave us with some keys, Carol. That's all we need to keep this show on the road!'

*   *   *

Three weeks before my leaving date, when we were in the throes of looking round the new vicarage and getting everyone together for Mark's priesting service at Short Heath, the telephone rang, and Bob the undertaker said, 'Lily Deakin, Carol? I understand she's one of yours.'

I swallowed, remembering my last visit to Lily when, as so often happens, we'd both known we were saying goodbye. 'I know she wanted to come to St Chad's,' I replied, opening my diary. 'So when are you thinking, Bob?'

The older man paused. 'That's a bit tricky, Carol,' he said. 'The next of kin is a niece from Cornwall, and she's saying the only convenient day for her is Wednesday!'

For a long time now I had been steering funerals away from Wednesdays because of the drop-in, realising that parking problems aside mourners wouldn't want to see the place full of sometimes disreputable looking characters, and that, for the drop-in clients too, having a hearse outside the door was hardly good for morale.

'I suppose at a push it could be Wednesday afternoon,' I compromised. 'About three?'

In my prayers that night I thanked God for Lily's life, and prayed that her service would be a celebration and a thanksgiving that would somehow touch the lives of others.

On the Wednesday, to my surprise, several of our regular clients stayed behind to help clear up – Stuart taking the board in unasked, and Janie Danks rather disjointedly pushing a broom around the floor.

'Talk about two worlds colliding,' I whispered to Frances, the verger, because as the undertakers went into the hall to have their customary cup of tea, a group of droppers-in still stood in silent respect where Lily's coffin had passed.

Afterwards, when I came back from the cemetery, I found Robbo Danks still standing with Peter and an almost unrecognisable Darren. Looking almost shame-faced, Robbo shuffled up to me, for all the world like a sick man in his late seventies instead of the middle-aged one that he was.

'It was a good funeral, Vicar. You give her a nice send off,' he said. Putting a skeletal hand up to his throat, he added, 'I was just wondering – would you bless these rosary beads? Ann's give 'em to me.'

*   *   *

On my final Sunday at St Chad's, I took my CD player into the church and played a lively song called 'Cast your burdens onto Jesus'. Demob happy, I tried to get everyone to move around, and was glad that faced with Fred's turned back and Audrey Freeman's penetrating glare, I at least had Claudia and Maureen who would respond.

Elizabeth Brown, an old friend and fellow woman priest, came along to the service saying she felt called to be with me. 'The last couple of years in this place have really taken their toll on you, Caz,' she said, hugging me when it was all over. 'I'm so glad you're getting away!'

Mixed emotions rose in me as I looked up at the crucifix suspended in the cold and dust high above us. I wondered what Wednesday would bring, a day I was both dreading and looking forward to.

As usual, the midweek communion was poorly attended, but as I began to follow Fred and his party out, I stopped dead in my tracks. There, right outside the portico doors, was a full-scale fairground hurdy-gurdy machine belting out loud cheery barrel organ music that could surely be heard right across Chadsmoor! It was attended by a man and a woman in bright, beaded clothes, and Mary was standing there, waving her thin arms about and declaring, 'Our Doreen got it! She knows somebody from the fair! Like it, Fred? Like it, Gladys?' Before they could reply, she had pushed them inside the hall for their coffee, and steered me towards the open street. 'You stay out here, Carol, and talk to folks as they go by! It's a really good advert! Lets the people know St Chad's is still here!'

The time passed as, rather puzzled, I did as I was told. In time, Fred and the ladies came out of the hall and left, giving me a perfunctory wave as they passed, just as if we'd all be meeting again the next time they came to church.

'That's that then,' I thought sadly, thinking back to the very apathetic send-off they'd given me after Sunday's evensong – an evensong Fred hadn't even attended.

I concentrated on talking to passers by and telling them about the barrel organ and inviting them to St Chad's. Around the church hall there was the usual activity: people arriving on foot or in cars, bringing their boxes, carrier bags and trays. All activities they didn't need me for.

The drop-in would continue. But what was it? Just glorified amateur social work? A free handout for the scum of society, who should be locked away? Some would certainly say so. But in the words Claudia had used in her Easter poem, Jesus said, 'Feed my sheep,' and the Wednesday drop-in didn't only feed them with food, it gave them love and companionship – and hope.

Suddenly, red-haired Larry appeared with his friend, Jordy. 'Shouldn't you be at school?' I asked.

Larry grinned. 'It's a teacher training day, and we heard the music!' he said.

As we stood chatting, more cars arrived so that the car park was full. Then Frank came out, calling cheerily, 'Hey, Carol. Where are you? Somebody wants to see you in the hall!'

The two boys followed me inside where, to my surprise, there were cameras flashing and a great cheer. Looking around, I couldn't take in what they'd done. There were balloons, streamers, special food, a table full of gifts, an iced cake, and a big banner that read 'Farewell to our Dancing Priest!'.

'Well, you said we were MAD, Caz!' Ann said, tearfully, amid all the hugs and kisses. 'But God shows MAD folk how to throw a party cos right from the start he's given us a banquet to share here, and he'll go on doing it, week after week!'

'Let's put some music on,' I gasped finally, after photographs were taken for the *Chase Telegraph* and we'd said our grace before the food.

'Just a minute!' As Tracy held her hands above her blonde head, I sensed something else had been pre-arranged. 'We thought you'd say that, so we've got a special song for you, haven't we, folks?'

Going to the player, she pressed a button and, puzzlingly, the sound of Lionel Richie filled the room. His words were soon drowned by the assembled, very motley, company singing together, 'You're once, twice, three times a vicar, and we l-o-o-o-o-v-e you!'

Through my tears and laughter, I recognised a blessing I would cherish for ever.

Postscript

St Chad's Wednesday drop-in continues to flourish, with an average attendance of between thirty and forty people. A Church Army captain has responsibility for the project, and the St Chad's vacancy is to be advertised as 'half-time'. Other churches in the area, and elsewhere in the Lichfield diocese, now offer similar support and outreach to addicts and others in need.

Useful Contacts

Alcoholics Anonymous
www.alcoholics-anonymous.org.uk
Tel: 0114 270 1984

Mothers Prayers
PO Box 822
Gravesend
Kent DA13 9ZZ
Tel: 01474 834084

Drinkline
Offers confidential, accurate and consistent information and advice on sensible drinking in line with government policy to anyone concerned about alcohol misuse, including people with alcohol problems, their families, friends and carers.
Tel: 0800 917 8282 (Mon-Fri 9.00 am - 11.00 pm;
Sat-Sun 6.00 pm - 11.00 pm)

The Kestrel Trust
A response to drug and alcohol dependence in the Christian Community.
PO Box 2742
Reading
RG4 6FN
Tel: 0118 947 8353

National Drugs Helpline

Offers confidential, accurate and consistent advice, information and support to anyone concerned about drug and solvent/volatile substance misuse, including drug misusers, their families, friends and carers.
Tel: 0800 77 66 00 (24 hrs)
Tel: 0800 917 6650 (Ethnic languages - wait for the language you want)

Narcotics Anonymous

A non-profit, international, community based organisation for recovering addicts that's active in over 60 countries. NA members learn from one another how to live drug free and recover from the effects of addiction in their lives.
www.ukna.org
Tel: 020 7730 0009

Release

Provides a range of services dedicated to meeting the health, welfare and legal needs of drugs users and those who live and work with them.
www.release.org.uk
Tel: 020 7729 9904

www.Drugs.gov.uk

The cross-government website to support the National Drugs Strategy and the work of Drug Action Teams. It is a one-stop shop for DATs and interested individuals to find out about the government's ten-year strategy.

Angels on the Walls

by Wallace and Mary Brown

What happens when a church drops its barricades against the community? Wallace and Mary Brown decided to do just that – literally. Situated in the middle of three large housing estates on the outskirts of Birmingham, with crime and vandalism all around, they stepped out in faith and took down the barbed wire and high walls. Gradually but unmistakably they saw their community begin to turn to Christ for healing and eternal life.

WALLACE & MARY BROWN

ANGELS ON THE WALLS

The risk-taking faith that reclaimed a community

CHURCH
alive

With refreshing honesty about the hard times as well as the rewarding times, this is the gripping story of how a small, defensive fellowship became a thriving church able to plant a new congregation in a neighbouring district.

CHURCH
alive